THE BIBLE AS
THE STORY OF YOU

THE BIBLE AS THE STORY OF YOU

A JOURNEY INTO LIGHT

JOHN LEE BAUGHMAN

DeVorss & Company, Publishers
1046 Princeton Drive
Marina del Rey, California 90291

ISBN: 0–87516–385–8
Library of Congress Card Catalog
Number: 79–54676

Printed in the United States of America
by Book Graphics, Inc., Marina del Rey, California

TO THE READER

This book is dedicated to ONE PURPOSE. That the reader may be able, henceforth, to read the Bible with an understanding of its OVERALL INTENT, and with a practical application of self to any of its INDIVIDUAL PARTS. Whether it be history, allegory, parable or promise.

Herein are contained SEVEN HIGHLIGHTS of the Old Testament and SEVEN HIGHLIGHTS of the New Testament—and done in such a manner *that anything in between is readily understood.* The FINAL CHAPTER deals with the PROMISES found in Both Testaments.

The main value of this book lies in its ability TO RELATE everything in the Bible TO YOU in such a way as to make it truly "A Journey Into Light" for your person.

CONTENTS

OLD TESTAMENT

OLD TESTAMENT

PART I.

"GENESIS, YOUR FRANCHISE TO LIFE."

"In the beginning God created the heaven
and earth."

"And the earth was without form, and void;
and darkness was upon the face of the deep.
And the Spirit of God moved upon the face of
the waters."

"And God said, Let there be light: and there
was light."

"And God said, Let the waters under the
heaven be gathered together unto one place,
and let the dry land appear: and it was so."

Genesis 1:1, 2, 3 and 9

Before I begin our subject, "Genesis, Your
Franchise to Life," I want to preface it with key
thoughts that will make it live. They will sort of
condition you.

Now this segment of the Bible, which I am
about to begin, makes no claim to being an

1

exhaustive study of the Old Testament. But it is done in such a way as to enable you to read the Old Testament with good, down-to-earth common sense.

In this segment, I must say, it does aim to show that the Bible is the story of you—in your journey into light. And that the Old Testament contains the first half of that story—all about you. Even though it takes up many events and many characters—every event and every character will have something to do with you.

To find yourself in this story I am about to tell, you must relate yourself to the event named and to the character described—to extract the inner meaning intended for you. Otherwise you read it in vain. That is what the metaphysical interpretation is all about, and this is a metaphysical interpretation of the Bible.

There are three kinds of information to look for and absorb: FIRST, there are of course, historical events as well as allegories and parables to be considered. In any case, you need to know that they are merely the "rack." Yes, whether it is an historical event or an allegory or a parable, it is merely the "rack" on which the "spiritual meat" is hung. Remember the great Biblical question, "Have ye any meat?" If you do not get the meat or spiritual meaning each episode relates to you, you have read in vain.

SECOND, the Bible is written in terms of man's unfoldment at the time each section of the Bible was written. In other words—his spiritual knowledge at that level—his superstitions at that level—and his morals at that level. If you look for and absorb what is being said and done at that particular level, you will find —what not to do in many instances. Why? Because it was simply the best man knew at that time—not something to be emulated. It could amount to outright superstition on some occasion, and downright immorality on another. The Bible tells it the way it is. It does not "whitewash" its heroes. You are to look for and weigh the ethics that are given—with the understanding they were the ethics at the level of man's unfoldment at that time.

The thing to look for here and absorb would be the spiritual meaning that each level in man's unfoldment depicts—the spiritual meaning to you. Why was it written? It was written to help you! "Job," for example, might help a great many more people than some of the more illumined souls of the Bible. Why? Because Job's experiences are pretty much like our own, you see. We understand him. There was hardly anything negative he missed. So look for the spiritual meaning that each level in man's unfoldment depicts. Look for it like the "treasure hid in the field," as the Bible puts it.

Now, there is a THIRD thing to look for and absorb in the Bible as we go along. It is something that is not an historical event, and not an allegory or a parable. That would be the Biblical promises that are strung from Genesis to Revelation. They are the greatest "concentrations" of spiritual meat in the Bible. Because each promise is a statement of Higher Law, containing a condition to be passed; and if you so pass it, a fruit to be enjoyed! That is the way to read the Biblical promises.

Some of the most uplifting promises are in the Old Testament. These promises or Higher Laws represent vital instruction, and you need to evaluate them for their worth. Always be open to the Biblical promise, whatever page it may happen to be on—for it has great spiritual meat for you.

Above all, remember that the Bible is a review of the gradual involution and evolution of the Spirit of God in man. That means the Bible is a review of the gradual involvement of the Spirit of God in your consciousness, and the gradual evolvement of it into form. That is the way the Bible is written. It is a journey into light. What I will deal with in our subject here is packed and crammed with the greatest Truth in depth you could possibly have. The rest of the Bible is spent in seeking to use it. And it is used at the level of the people involved in each instance.

That the Bible is the story of the gradual involvement in man of God's Spirit and the evolvement of it into form is obvious through the FOUR DISTINCT STEPS man experiences in the first half of his story found in the Old Testament. Now you know, if we had a motion picture here, I would be doing for it—what I am doing for you in the Bible. I am going to tell you what is going to happen—four steps you can look for in the Old Testament. And remember, it is a story about you.

The FIRST STEP begins on the high note of the creation of Spiritual Man. This is what you may refer to as your God Self or Deeper Self or True Self or Real Self. Here is the explanation of this Spiritual Self in depth, that is rarely ever presented.

The SECOND STEP moves to the activity of this Spiritual Man in you—forming manifest man—the outer Adam man of you or intellectual man with free will.

The THIRD STEP records man's departure from God through misuse of free will. It is known as the "fall of man." You have heard of that, have you not? Most people remember the negative things better than the great things in the Bible. "The fall of man? Oh yes, I know that one," they say. But their knowledge of it is amusing, to say the least. And I shall tell you why! They think the cause of all our trouble today is due to Adam and Eve "falling" way back then. But Adam and Eve is just a parable.

And a parable is just a fictitious story, depicting, in this instance, the misuse of your intellectual (Adam) and emotional (Eve) natures through free will—a "falling away" from God's will then or NOW!

In the rest of the Old Testament—the FOURTH STEP—you will find man's gradual efforts toward regeneration. Spiritual man— the individualized presence of God in you— when you really grasp it, truly regenerates. You lost it, whenever you "fell" away from His Truth. And now you realize "falling away" from your Spiritual Self or Real Self really does not offer anything except all kinds of trouble. So for the rest of the story you are really trying to regenerate yourself. That is what the Old Testament is all about. The remaining part of the Old Testament is your attempt or man's attempt, through gradual efforts, to find his lost Eden— the Eden out of which he kicked himself.

Finally, in receiving the Old Testament, which is about to follow, know this: The seeds of Truth, that came to fruitage in the New Testament, were sown in the Old Testament.

That we cannot fully understand or even appreciate the New Testament—without a knowledge of the great growth in man's unfoldment contained in the Old Testament.

Before we begin the first half of your story in the Old Testament, I want to emphasize this: We are not in reality Hebrew or Christian or whatever. We are one people headed toward one goal—to make God manifest! You and I shall not be satisfied until we awake from our stupor with beholding His form expressed—that which He wants done!

All this has just been a preface. Now we are going to get down to real business. Are you ready? Do not grasp your chair, tense up and say, "This is going to be deep, and over my head." Just relax. We are going to make the deepest Truths simple.

Our subject is, "Genesis, Your Franchise To Life." If I had wanted to make our subject even more detailed I could have called it, "Genesis, Your Franchise To The More Abundant Life in The Spot You Occupy." And that would be the Truth!

The Bible opens with the words, "In the beginning God." You would be surprised how many times over the years I have heard this question, "Well, what happened before that?" Frankly, such people do not know how to read the Bible. If you read it metaphysically, you read behind the scenes and you get the point, which the Bible wants to make to you. And the point here is, "In the beginning—THAT NEVER BEGAN—God."

Now you think about that. It will clear your head fast. "In the beginning that never began, God." And using the same premise of spiritual reasoning, "In the beginning that never began, you"—as part of His manifesting nature. Does that stun you? Does that shock you? Oh, you were not in the form that you presently are. You have gone through many stages of evolution. But still you were a definite identity in the manifesting side of God. You were that. That is your nature, you know—the manifesting nature of God. That is what you have always been. That kind of makes you sit up and take notice, does it not? Because most people have never delved into this at all. To stretch the boundaries of your consciousness, consider the following set of passages from Proverbs 8:22, 26, 27, "The Lord possessed me in the beginning of His way . . . While as yet He had not made the earth (with its evolution) . . . When He prepared the heavens, I was there: . . ."

Let us consider a little form of spiritual reasoning in a syllogism form—a syllogism of spiritual logic. Most religious people profess to believe in eternal life as belonging to the individual. Many go to church for that reason. They say, "Got to get my share of this business of going on, you know." That is the big item with them. But did you ever stop to think—that what is eternal can have no beginning, any more than it can have an ending?

Here is a strange thing about the way the human being reasons. He knows he was born. That he sprang into being, you see. That is all he remembers. So he sprang into being—seemingly from nothing. And now he believes he belongs to eternal life. But if he believes that he belongs to eternal life, he must also believe he always was. This is the missing link of spiritual reasoning he overlooks. It may come as a "shocker" to you. I am going to keep on shocking you. In other words, eternity is a "two-way stretch." Applied to self it amounts to this: If you believe in eternal life for yourself, then you must believe you always were. Eternity cannot have just one end!

Human birth was not the beginning of you, merely your entrance to this plane. On this much you can count. You did not start at birth. The Bible says you were what? Created equal in an "image and likeness." Yet no two here started equal at birth. You were created equal, but at birth you may have been blind. I almost was. Some were a "blue baby," a common parlance description for one without proper circulation. Some were born in miserable circumstances. Some in happy circumstances. Yet we were created equal. Where does that leave us? Frankly, we had to do some living before we got here. And I am not writing about reincarnation—just the ongoing you!

What is the practical application of this great point we are now making? "In the beginning, God" and "in the beginning, you" as His manifesting nature. For every day of your life, "In the beginning" of every project in your life from now on—God. The way you approach it is, "In the beginning of this project, I, as a Truth student, must have this feeling: God is the First Causation of this whole process. He stands behind me, and I am the manifesting nature of His Causation."

Talk about going back to your Real Self. This is an inside picture of it. He is First Causation, and you—the manifesting nature of First Causation. No secondary causations—nothing of this world to stop you or hold you back. The Bible backs it up. It says, ". . . Let there be light: . . ." (Genesis 1:3). The application here is that "light" for that project is the idea from God. That is what First Causation is—the idea, the "know-how," the "do it absolutely right." The Bible goes on to say, ". . . and let the dry land appear: . . ." (Genesis 1:9). In other words, let the idea come into form. But you must be the manifesting nature, and your part is to let the idea come into form from God!

Now the Bible condenses the whole story of creation into less than 600 words. Yes, Genesis does it in about 600 words, while the theory of evolution uses hundreds of volumes. Are they so different? I dare say that most people would say, "Oh yes, they are quite different. One believes we evolved from minute forms of life; the other that we descended from God. Never can these two philosophies agree." Not at all. They actually tell the same story.

I was amused on hearing a person in this field in another part of the country say, "It is more or less verified today that we came up through the evolutionary pattern," and left it hanging there. I thought to myself, I can excuse lay people for such a view. But for a man supposedly giving himself to total research in a specialized field— he certainly is off base in his information. Obviously he lacked the Key.

Let me tell you the words in the Bible that give you the key. So never again will you be bothered with this subject. The words in Genesis are these. I have picked them out for you. They really unite the two theories, if you want to call them theories—the theory of Genesis and the theory of evolution. The first words are these, ". . . Which the waters brought forth abundantly, AFTER THEIR KIND. . . ." (Genesis 1:21). You know in evolution all forms

of life came from the water. And then moved
forth upon the land.

So you see, Genesis says the same thing ". . .
which the waters brought forth abundantly,
AFTER THEIR KIND . . ." and then in Genesis
1:24, it says, ". . . Let the earth bring forth the
living creature AFTER HIS KIND. . . ." What
is it saying both times? After the seed idea in
which each species was created by God—first in
water, then on land!

Now I am a research man myself, and one of
the things, which it has always pleased me to
relate to others, is that the search for the earliest
evidence of man's existence on earth continues
unabated. You can go over to the Museum of
Natural History in New York City and review
various forms of man—at certain stages in his
unfoldment.

But here is the beauty. Way back there, when
those reproductions you have reviewed were
real beings on this plane—were part of the
species known as man—there was also a type
walking right along side of him, which was an

ape! That, they did not tell you about at the museum. But that is what Genesis is correctly saying, "Each species after its kind." Do not let anyone ever tell you that you are the product and the present left-over of a once form of ape life. Read the following scientific report carefully:

"JERUSALEM, Israel (AP)—The accepted view on evolution of man from the ape is absolutely incorrect and without any scientific basis, anthropologist Louis Leakey said at the Israel Academy of Science and Humanities.

"Giving new details in a lecture of his recent discoveries in Kenya which he said throw light on the origin of mankind, Dr. Leakey states that, while the chimpanzee is man's cousin in blood groups and other factors, the human race did not descend from the ape in a way accepted in the past.

"Leakey told a news conference in Nairobi recently that the remains unearthed in Rusinga Island in Lake Victoria date back 20 million years or more. He said he sees in them bone fragments of proto-man, by far and away the oldest known representatives of the stock which eventually gave rise to man.

"Thus Leakey disputed the accepted scientific view that man developed from the baboon from 3 to 5 million years ago.

"There was no sudden rush of evolution from the ape to man in a mere 5 million years, he said. Remains were found proving that apes, 20 to 25 million years ago, were developing in the direction in which apes are still today. But at that time, proto-man, our ancestor, already existed."

All of which is in keeping with the inspired writings found in Genesis!

Yes, in you is the seed idea of man, as distinct from all other seeds of life. And as a descendant of that particular creation, you were given dominion over all the lesser forms. Dominion over them does not mean to dominate them. Rather to call forth that which is divinely natural in them. And when you do that, then the Bible says that all the various forms of life—the lion and the lamb—shall lie down together.

That is the real story. It does not refute evolution—it unites it with the involution of the Spirit of God—if you have the key. The attempt of Hebrew authors to explain God and man—was put together following Babylonian captivity—toward the end of Hebrew history covering 4,000 years. The Old Testament is a collection of writings that were saved and put together at a later date. Will you remember that? They were saved. They were written at different times, but they were saved. And they were put together after the Babylonian captivity, which is nearly at the end of Hebrew history in the Bible.

Let me give you a sample of this. The second chapter of Genesis was written first, and the first chapter of Genesis was written second in the time slot. As a matter of fact, the first chapter of Genesis was written over four centuries after the second chapter was written.

Now, if that bothers you, let me put it to you this way: Most people read the first two chapters of Genesis and say, "What's with all this redundancy? This repeating itself. The second chapter sounds like the first. And the first sounds like the second." No, you simply do not know how to read them. Some scholars even thought that the Hebrews had two versions of Genesis. Not at all.

The deep Truth to learn here is that the first chapter is God doing the whole thing—IN MIND. It is like building a house as a contractor or architect; you would do it in mind first. The second chapter is the same thing all over again, but now COMING INTO FORM, including man. Also, the first three paragraphs of the second chapter belong to the first chapter. Why? Obviously they were not too knowledge-able in separating chapters in those days. In any event, that is the way to read the two chapters.

Now in the original language of the Bible— not found in our translations—three terms, forming a trinity, are used to explain God and man. They are Elohim God, Jehovah God and Adam. Elohim God, means God everywhere equally present. Jehovah God, means His indi-vidualization in man. And Adam, means intel-lectual man with free will, formed by Jehovah God as a vehicle through which to express Him-self on this plane. As Adam or intellectual man, with free will, learns only to do the will of God, he would then become transformed into Jehovah God, which has the same meaning as Christ in the New Testament.

However, it needs to be pointed out here that the Judaeo-Christian Bible is only one of many bibles in the world. And it is safe to say that nearly all people of the many civilizations of the past have theorized as to their beginnings.

So the Hebrew narrative of creation, however inspired we believe it to be—as to who we are, why we are, and where we are going—remains a theory along with the other bibles—unless proven.

This is the role of Jesus Christ. He was living proof for both Hebrews and Christians alike that the spiritual thesis espoused by Genesis was accurate.

Jesus was the first Adam man, at least of whom we have record, who completely transcended the human self and became Jehovah God of the Old Testament or Christ of the New Testament. Both terms, of course, mean exactly the same thing—God individualized in man and manifesting His own pure ideas into form.

Moses, Elijah, Elisha were great demonstrators in this direction and thus contributed, and were also wayshowers to—what Jesus was finally able to do.

Let us take note here of how Jesus acted out the spiritual thesis of Genesis to the last decimal. He claimed "One is greater than I, even the Father," meaning Elohim God.

Then He claimed to be the Son of God, meaning the individualization of God in man or Jehovah God or Christ. But He claimed this also for every man, referring to the Old Testament passage from Psalms 82:6, "Ye are gods, and all of you children of the Most High."

Finally, in His immortal Lord's Prayer, He made clear that, "God's will must be done in earth as it is in heaven," citing what Adam must do. Thus you see, you truly have the spiritual thesis of Genesis proved out to the last decimal.

Why? Through position of Sonship, and from

it, Jesus overcame every malformation He met along the highway of life with true formation— be it in the body, human relations or finances— even to the last enemy or last malformation, death itself.

And what is more, He said to you from that same position ". . . the works that I do shall he (you) do also . . ." (John 14:12).

Thus, Genesis IS your franchise to the "life more abundant" in the spot you occupy. But it remains with you to exercise that franchise!

Spiritual Meditation

In the beginning that never began, GOD. And by like token of spiritual reasoning, in the beginning that never began, YOU, as a part of His Manifesting Nature. Oh, not in your present form do you fully reveal this. You have evolved through many crude forms of such a Spiritual Man, always intuitively seeking to become in form what you already are. What is that? Even as Elohim God (Father or Source) created Jehovah God (Spiritual Man) to be His Manifesting Nature; even so did Jehovah God create

Adam man (Outer man) to be His vehicle on this plane.

How does the Bible put it? "Beloved, now are we the Sons of God, and it doth not yet appear (in form) what we shall be . . ." (1 John 3:2). The slowness of your evolvement has been due to your free will as intellectual man, Adam. But even as that outer self was originally created and thus intended to be a vehicle for Jehovah God; even so that divine seed of you will not be denied. As David put it, "I shall be satisfied when I awake with Thy likeness." (Psalms 17:15).

Yes, eventually the Adam man of you will learn that his own final and complete freedom lies in doing solely the will of your Real Self or Spiritual Man. Then Adam man in you will transcend himself and become in form what Jehovah God already is—the Manifesting Nature or Executor of what Elohim God wants done!

". . . My Father worketh hitherto, and I work." (John 5:17)

OLD TESTAMENT

PART II.

"YOUR ETERNAL CREATIVE PROCESS"

". . . , Let there be light: . . ."
>
> Genesis 1:3

". . . , Let there be a firmament in the midst of the waters . . ."
>
> Genesis 1:6

"Let the waters under the heaven be gathered into one place, and let the dry land appear: . . ."
>
> Genesis 1:9

"Let there be lights in the firmament of the heaven to divide the day from the night; . . ."
>
> Genesis 1:14

(Plus Genesis 1:20 and 24, Genesis 2:1 and 3)

Our subject, "Your Eternal Creative Process," is the second highlight in the series on the Old Testament. It tells us of the process by which you should work out every new and better thing for your life—once you have taken your correct position in the scheme of things.

Most people have no notion of their true position. Therefore, much of their lives works against the current. They are going upstream instead of with the current of God. The original language of the Bible, of which you have only translations, gives the most detailed account of your position possible. So that you can be aligned with your God once again.

Never underestimate that. Because if you know anything about sports, whatever the sport, the first thing to learn is position. In tennis, you would do yourself proud taking instruction to learn position. Otherwise you will be a poor player for the rest of your life. No matter how endowed you may be as a natural athlete.

In golf, you would do yourself justice to learn position, also. Otherwise the same—you remain a "hacker." It is true of all games. It is true of life; because life, too, is a game, and you need to learn position to play it properly. The Old Testament at its outset, gives you the most thorough description of position to be found.

As I said in the first chapter of this book, our Judaeo-Christian Bible is only one of many bibles in the world, and perhaps most races of antiquity had their Genesis—how they theorized their beginnings. But what makes the Judaeo-Christian Genesis unique is that it no longer remains a spiritual thesis or theory. Why? Because the keys in it have been utilized and proven in complete demonstration over every malformation in life—by such way-showers as Moses, Elijah, Elisha—and finished by Jesus. And what has been done by men, any other man then can do by working the same way from correct position. So in Genesis you do have your franchise for the "life more abundant" in the spot you occupy.

Genesis largely sets up that position. Whether Genesis was done by one writer or a group— the original language here is detailed. The writer (or writers) certainly was a great metaphysician. For he describes God, our everywhere-equally-present Father, as Elohim God.

You could never be that. Because you are the Son, the individualization of Him in the spot you occupy. So you need a distinct realization of our Over-All Father God or Source, and the Hebrew narrative names it—Elohim God.

Then it makes clear that our everywhere-equally-present God ensouled Himself in you. Individualized Himself as Jehovah God. And that is the description of the Spiritual Man of you. Perfect, because it is the individualization of the perfection of God. Such is that to which you like to repair and call your Real Self or Deeper Self. Here you have a detailed account of it. That is Jehovah God, Spiritual Man, the Executor of God. Thus you are the intended Executor of God in the spot you occupy.

Now, the Adam man of you—the outer man —was made by this Jehovah God or Spiritual Man. This individualization of God, you see, needed a vehicle through which to manifest or express on this plane. Thus the outer you was created. The name for that in the original language, as well as the translation you own, is Adam. And the meaning of this outer you is that you were given an intellect, and in that intellect

—free will. So you do not have to go with God. But you make a mistake, if you do not. Why? Because you tie yourself into knots.

So in time you must learn that the only true free will is when you have learned to live utterly by the will of God, and want just that will of God done. Know once and for all, that the will of God contains in no instance in your eternity —one negative. It is totally positive. If you do not know that for sure, you are far back in your knowledge of Truth.

That is the picture. That is your position. So in walking down the street of life, you should know that your everywhere-equally-present Father, Elohim God—over Australia as well as where you are—is intimately related to you. Having individualized Himself in you as Jehovah God, He then created this outer you, Adam. And when you learn to do only the will of Him who sent you, this Adam self will transcend himself and become the Spiritual Man or Jehovah God, the Executor of all that the Father is.

Now we are going to try it out here with our Father's "Eternal Creative Process," which is the correct follow thru of your position as His Son. We are going to try it out on one thing— your problem of the moment. In this "process," you are going to seek to transcend your outer self and become totally this individualization— this Spiritual Man or Jehovah God. At least as far as this problem is concerned, you are going to work completely with God. Are you willing to try it? When you get one thing done through this "process," you will be ready to move forward as never before on all other things.

So you have your major problem of the moment. That is nobody's business but your own. But it is very important that you face it. This is nature's way of telling you where to go to work, and you are going to let seven movements of God take place in you. In letting those seven movements take place through you, there is no way in which this problem can stand on its own two feet any longer. Nothing can withstand the pressure of these seven movements of God!

People like to call those seven movements, the Seven Days of Creation. Thus, that being something they know, their tendency is to toss it off, saying, "Oh, yes, I know that." But you do not really know this process personally, until you know it to be seven distinct movements that need to come through you to wipe out any problem, and use it to release the dominion of God for your particular problem of the moment. Ready to try it?

I cannot set you up with your problem. You have already had somebody do that, namely yourself. But to make this practical—face it! Together we are going to give it back to God. All right?

Now Elohim God is the Source of all divine ideas. And this Presence is the Source of the idea you need for this case. Thus the idea lies in the individualization or Jehovah God of you. And the Adam or outer self of you says, "I am willing to let that idea take over." Yes, you are so willing, that you are going to transcend yourself as far as this problem is concerned, and become Jehovah God or God individualized in you— what He would do here!

Understanding the Seven Days of Creation

for you represent seven movements of God in your mind, you are now letting the first movement take over—as far as your problem is concerned.

The first step or movement from God, is "Let there be light." (Genesis 1:3). Meaning at this precise moment you are letting the idea that originates only from God possess your intellect. How? You are Truth student enough to know what you belong to there in God—generally speaking. For your body, only wholeness—if that is your problem. For your human relations, only harmony—if that is your problem. For your finances, only supply—if that is your problem. Yes, you are Truth student enough to know what you belong to there in God.

So that is the beginning of laying hold of the idea from God. You are "seeing what the Father is doing" there now. What He wants done. Again, you are Truth student enough to know what He is doing. And this is that which you are "seeing." At this very moment, then, God is beginning in you, His idea about your problem.

And the end shall be as the beginning. There

shall be a spiritual working out as God wants it from this idea. Why? Because you have the idea only of what God wants done there. In your free will you are willing that this possess you. Thus you are possessed of this idea—only what God wants done there!

The second step or the second movement from God is, "Let there be a firmament in the midst of the waters." The way to decipher any biblical passage is through its polar words or sometimes polar phrases. The polar words here are "firmament" and "waters." Let us see how they give us the meaning of this second movement.

Now you have started with an idea in your intellect, the idea of what God wants done. But you know that it will not demonstrate until the idea becomes a part of your feeling nature. Why? Because you only demonstrate your feelings—your subconscious mind. The conscious mind cannot demonstrate a "thin dime." So you are now told to let this idea become "firmament" or firm in the midst of your waters. The second polar word, "waters," means your feeling nature. Let the idea become firm there.

So claim, then, that you are beginning to feel this unexpressed possibility—the idea of what God wants done here. That it is becoming firm or sure in your feeling nature. In this second step, you are having the growing sense of surety and firm conviction that as you go through these seven movements the problem has to go.

This new firmness, this new surety in your feeling nature about what God wants done there—is your new faith. So there is a new faith in you. A firm surety that this is going to work out.

Now the third step or the third movement from God is, "Let the waters be gathered in one place. . . ." The polar words that decipher this are "waters," "gathered" and "place." "Waters," means your feelings, that are now firm and sure in their faith, must be "gathered" in one "place." I often say, "It is like taking a gob of butter and putting it on one spot." Your knowledge of Truth must no longer remain general, you see. You want the application of all the Truth you know on this one thing. Like a gob of butter you are putting it on this one spot, so you can taste it. All your feelings are gathered there.

Firm, sure feelings as to what God wants done there. And that it is going to happen!

It goes on to say, "Let the dry land appear." "Dry land" is the third polar key. "Dry land" obviously means the result. Means let the working out of what God wants done take place. Yes, you received the idea or way out from God. You let it become a sure conviction in your feelings. You gathered these firm feelings together in one place—on your problem. You are asked now to let the "dry land"— what God wants done there—appear or come into manifestation.

Basically, what is the new thing you are doing in this third movement? You are shaping this idea from God, by the formative activity of your intellect. And the formative activity of your intellect is your imagination. You are now "seeing" in advance the working out into form. Your imagination, acting like scissors, is cutting this idea into a pattern. You are seeing in form the finished working out—in this third movement. You are shaping your idea to that, but leaving the details as to how—to God.

It is becoming very definite for your body, for example. You no longer have a case of bad stomach, heart or kidney. You have a boiled down picture of a perfectly functioning stomach, heart or kidney. That is your new picture.

Now if your problem was the sale of something—in your imagination you have the sale. Remaining with the problem amounts to—no sale. So in your imagination you behold the great movement of God not only upon you but also upon all persons having anything to do with the sale—leading and prompting all to the final consummation of the sale. Yes, God is bringing the perfect buyer in His own way. All this is a part of your picture. You live in joyous anticipation of the finished working out. Meanwhile, taking all the outer steps that come to you to do.

Then, if your problem is one of human relations—in your imagination see only the picture of wonderful harmony there, no longer the problem. Imagine the picture being filled in by nothing less than God himself—bringing forgiveness, bringing harmony, bringing love, bringing an orderly working out—correcting you and all persons involved. That is all you see. You have the sense of God's Holy Spirit moving upon all. The feeling that nothing and no one can withstand its holy pressure putting things right.

If your problem lies in the area of work and finances, have your next true place of service pictured in your imagination as already established—with you in it. Know that God has already prepared it in advance, and is taking you to it. The same for your increase. Include in your picture the great Truth that "sufficiency and to spare" is the Higher Law of your finances. See it, crystal clear, as being already established. And see yourself in it. Now you have passed the third movement.

The fourth step or movement from God is, "Let there be lights in the firmament . . . to divide the day from the night." This is from Genesis 1:14. Let us understand here that every passage in the Bible has levels of depth. When you read the Bible you are reading a book of keys or symbols. Each is as deep as you are ready to receive. Now you are after something deeper than its surface meaning, which obviously is—the dividing of day from night. Let us individualize it to your case.

The polar words are "lights" and "firmament." Yes, "lights" for this new "firmness" of faith you now have about your working out— new lights in this firmament. Beyond the idea, the original idea you started out with earlier. Where I said you were enough of a Truth student to know what God wants there in your body, human relations and finances in a general way. Now you need added light. These added lights will make your faith even more understanding for this working out.

The two great lights important here are understanding and will. The Bible says in effect, "He that keepeth understanding shall find (the) good" (he is after). As far as will is concerned, it is made abundantly clear in the Lord's Prayer that a great key to living is to let, "God's will be done."

So the two additional lights that are important here to add to your faith are—understanding and willingness. Let me say this. Understanding is not enough, unless it is tied to spiritual willingness—not will power but spiritual willingness. Even as will does not reach its full power for God until it is grounded in spiritual understanding.

So you have these two great lights. Use them to make your faith ever greater. Keep on understanding, in this fourth movement, that the working out is inevitable. And be oh so willing, oh so willing that this happen. Not will power, your willingness here should be like a mechanical lathe holding a block of wood in place. The highest use of will lies in holding the idea of what God wants done—in place. Not trying to force it to happen yourself by will power, but by simply holding it up to God for His power to do it. Keep understanding, then, that your working out is definitely going to take place, and be oh so willing by holding it up to God. Now your faith is even more potent for releasing the action of God to get the needed result done.

The fifth step or movement from God is, "Let the waters swarm with swarms of living creatures; and let the birds fly above the earth."

(Genesis 1:20). The new polar keys here that give meaning as to the relationship of this movement to you are "living creatures" and "birds."

Then to get to the meaning of this fifth movement. Every statement of the Bible has a surface meaning and a meaning in depth—the meaning in depth that pertains to your life now. The surface statement merely means that many kinds of marine life were now formed in the waters as well as other forms of life in the skies. But the meaning for you is that you are now letting something happen in your feeling nature (waters)—above and beyond the steps you have taken to date.

In other words, you are letting additional thoughts from God, pertinent to the working out of your problem, swarm into your feeling nature. Why? Because you are gently and persistently continuing to pray. So you are letting God continue to tell you by talking to you. And God talks to you how? By "a still, small voice." And "a still, small voice" is what? Not English, Spanish or Portuguese—it is an inner prompting.

As you continue to let the movements of God

compile themselves here, "swarms of living creatures"—more than ever—come to you. More thoughts, I should say, about the original idea, more thoughts come to you embellishing your "know how." Yes, you are allowing now for more thoughts from God to come to you and embellish the original idea of what God wants done in your case. You should be seeing more, then, expecting more than ever. So more thoughts will keep coming in to you to round out the original idea.

This makes the original idea of what God wants done even more alive. "And birds fly above the earth." "Birds," the other key, means somewhat the same thing. You are now reaching full understanding about the original idea from God. "Birds" represent thoughts approaching spiritual understanding. They are above earthly thought, and carry your mind upward toward the higher realm of Spirit.

Now we come to the sixth step, or the sixth movement from God. It says, "Let the earth bring forth living creatures after his kind." And God said, "Let us make man in our image, after our likeness." These are the two passages I have

put as one for the sixth step. (Genesis 1, verses
24 and 27). This is the meaning. "Earth" is a
polar word. "His kind" is a polar key. Then let
us come back to you being made on this sixth
day. "Man" is a polar word. How is he made?
In an "image and likeness." That is the other
polar key.

Now let us see how pertinent that is—this
sixth movement. We are getting close to the
end. Earth is your expressed world. Even as the
fifth step said, "Let your feelings (water) swarm
with this additional embellishment . . ." Even
so, now the sixth step says, "Let the earth bring
forth . . . after his kind." And earth is what?
Your expressed world.

Then, let us return to you. You were made on
this sixth day or by this sixth movement. God
made you in His image and likeness—the spiritual man first, then manifest man following into
form. This is a good illustration: Why? Even so
now, the thing that is happening in your life—
that which God wants done—is the form that is
about to appear. And this form shall be exactly
in keeping with its idea in God. Just as an image
and likeness idea first formed the spiritual you,

and then the manifest you. So this current thing with you, its working out—will be exactly in keeping with the idea God had for it. It has been embellished, rounded out and now it is going to be produced into form. Why will this take place? Because you have allowed six movements to move upon you from God.

What were they? First, you let the pure idea from God possess your mind. Second, you let it become firm in your feelings—so that you have a firm, new faith. Third, you let this idea take shape in your imagination, peculiar to your needs. Fourth, you added understanding and willingness to your new faith. Fifth, you let additional thoughts from God embellish the original idea.

Now you have come to the Sixth Movement. Here you are knowing the working out of your current need must come into form in your earth —in your expressed world. And after the original image and likeness idea for it. Even though that idea has been embellished and rounded out. Yes, you now know your demonstration simply must come into form in your earth—in your manifest world. And after the original image and likeness for it—the idea from God—plus His additional embellishing thoughts to round it out. In other words, the end is going to be as the beginning—as God wanted it—His working out.

Finally you come to the wonderful Seventh Movement. This seventh step or movement from God is, "And God rested on the seventh day from all His work which He had made." (Genesis 2:1 and 3). This holds the final requirement. Its first polar word is "rested." The other polar key is "from all His works."

Let me put it this way to you: Do not underestimate this last step. It has an exact movement in it, the same as the other six. And it is all important to your final demonstration. Here it is: Having done your part—the first six steps, allowing these first six movements to become you—"Rest in Jehovah and wait patiently for Him." That is the seventh and final step.

Now this waiting patiently, which you are starting to do, does not mean being inactive. It means living in a quiet state of confident expectancy that all that is necessary to complete this particular demonstration is being done.

You have gone after your demonstration boldly, knowing that you have infinite resources behind you. You shall now find these resources closing around you, and coming to your aid. Having done your part, you can depend upon God to do His. And that means take it the rest of the way!

Spiritual Meditation

The Seven Days of Creation represent seven movements of mind in man through which God creates continuously from the ideal into the formed. Even as God created you in His image and likeness to be His manifesting nature, even so then He continues to express His images or ideas (larger and better concepts of life) through you eternally. "Eye hath not seen nor ear heard the things which I have in store for them that love Me," as the Bible puts it.

First, let there be the idea in your mind of the new and better thing God wants done through you. ("Behold, I will do a new thing; now it shall spring forth; shall ye not know it.")

Second, let your feelings about that idea become firm or sure (faith).

Third, let your imagination (scissors of the mind that cuts the idea into a pattern) shape that idea in your mind.

Fourth, keep understanding this new and better thing is coming into your life, and keep willing (The two great lights important here are understanding and willingness).

Fifth, continue to let God talk to you (promptings or feelings from within) about that original idea and show you further how to bring it into form.

Sixth, know that it now must come into form only after God's original idea and embellishing thoughts, that the end may be as the beginning.

Seventh, finally and lastly rest upon God's Grace or Higher Action to bring it about. (Do not underestimate this last step.)

OLD TESTAMENT

PART III.

"ADAM AND EVE, CLARIFIED AND MADE PRACTICAL"

"And the man (Adam) said, The woman (Eve) whom Thou gavest to be with me, she gave me of the tree, and I did eat. And the Lord God said unto the woman, What is this thou hast done? And the woman said, the serpent beguiled me. . . ."   Genesis 3:12 and 13

"And the Lord had respect unto Abel and to his offering but unto Cain and to his offering he had not respect . . . Cain rose up against Abel, his brother, and slew him."

Genesis 4:4, 5 and 8

"But with thee (Noah) will I establish My covenant; and thou shalt come into the ark . . . and of every living thing of all flesh, two of every sort. . . ."

Genesis 6:18 and 19

"And they said . . . Let us build us . . . a
tower, whose top may reach unto heaven; and
let us make us a name . . . and the Lord said,
. . . confound their language . . . therefore is
the name of it (tower) called Babel."

Genesis 11:4,6,7 and 8

Our subject is "Adam and Eve, Clarified And
Made Practical." This is the third high light in
the series on the Old Testament.

"Adam and Eve" is the greatest parable in the
entire Bible. Why? Because it is the foundation
for the rest of the Bible. The rest of the Bible
assumes an understanding on your part of this
parable. From here on you will be in the process
of getting such an understanding, because you
are going to start it right now.

Showing the influence of this particular parable over the spread of the entire Bible, it is
interesting to note that it is mentioned even
toward the end of the Bible in Revelation. Do
you know what Revelation really is? It is a
depiction of your experiences to come, experiences you have never had as yet—a continuance
of the plan of God.

Yes, even in Revelation, which is the last chapter in the New Testament, this particular parable is referred to still. Interesting? As a matter of fact, it is spoken of quite graphically. For example, it speaks of the future of man in which he at long last finds his lost Eden. Why? Because he is finally conditioned to eat no longer of the "tree of good and evil," which has been his great mistake, but only of the "tree of life" itself. Obviously a processing is necessary to be able to eat properly of the "tree of life."

The particular reference made to the "tree of life" in Revelation is found in Revelation 22:2, ". . . The leaves of the tree were for the healing of the nations." Therefore, the parable of "Adam and Eve" is certainly a "must" to understand, to get clear in your mind and to make practical in your life. It holds real values for any searching soul. This parable tells how man, designed to work in at one ment with God, falls from that high estate. So this parable is also known as the "Fall of Man."

In the rest of the Old Testament we view man's efforts toward regeneration. His attempts to find his lost Eden again. And I have already referred to the point that he finally does so in

Revelation—referring to experiences we have not yet had but still remain for us in the plan of God.

The first thing to get straight about the Story of Adam and Eve is that it is just a parable, and a parable is a fictitious story depicting a great Truth. Thus it is not to be taken as historical fact. Do you understand? If you do not, you will shortly. Yes, this is a parable, therefore not to be taken literally. What a lot of rubbish that throws into the proverbial ashcan—religiously speaking. Why do so many people think about the story of Adam and Eve as though it were something that happened in the course of history? They are helped into this concept by motion pictures—scenario writers in particular. But it is not their fault. Their business is to project an image. And the one given them is the popular image suggested by religion.

So people run around mentally, following this kind of image in their minds: Adam was the first man on earth. One could get ten points on his scorecard for that. And Eve was made out of his rib. One could get another ten points for that. Adam and Eve found themselves in the Garden of

Eden. That gives one another possible ten points. And this was located somewhere in the Mesopotamia Valley. Oh, that is extra special. One probably could get fifteen points for that. Then Eve ate, and got Adam also to eat an apple, which was forbidden by God. And this caused both of them, both Adam and Eve, to be kicked out of the Garden of Eden. That is bad enough. But having happened—these two, way back then, caused all the misery and all the trouble that man has had ever since. One should get the most points of all for that!

All of which is what some people walk around with in their religious thinking. They actually believe that. Nothing could be more ridiculous. It is a parable. A little bit of common sense should tell you that if these two people wanted a bit of trouble—and got it—their trouble should not be passed on to all others during the years since.

Here we come to the interesting part. How can you be sure it was a parable? After all, are you supposed to take my word for it? I am just a researcher after the Truth. No! You go by the evidence. If you had no other evidence than the fact that the "deadly tree" in this story was not an apple tree, as people usually suppose, but a "tree of good and evil," it would be enough. Never was it an apple tree, no matter how many times it has been erroneously portrayed as such.

Now have you ever seen a literal "tree of good and evil" in anyone's backyard lately? Well, of course not. If you have, I would not tell anyone about it. It would be like telling people you have recently seen rain falling up instead of down. Obviously, then, there being no such thing as a literal "tree of good and evil," we have a parable here.

Consider again what a parable is. A parable is a fictitious narrative—from which a great spiritual Truth is drawn. That is simple, is it not? Yes, a fictitious story from which a great spiritual Truth is drawn. All right, what is an allegory? It is much the same. It is a description of one thing under the image of another—in which the actions are symbolic of the other's actions.

Now the only difference that I can see between a parable and an allegory is that a parable is based upon a fictitious story. While an allegory bases its story upon some factual commonplace thing known to everyone; then draws a parallel from it to a great spiritual Truth. So while similar they are different, and I think that is rather helpful because of what I am about to say—which is quite important!

The first eleven chapters of Genesis present a number of allegories and parables. Meaning the persons and the events mentioned in the stories are not necessarily actual or historical. Yet they depict supreme spiritual Truths that affect all men everywhere for all generations. Thus they offer you much to consider. Depicting tremendous spiritual Truths about you—is their total purpose!

The allegory of the creation of "Spritual Man" is found in the first chapter of Genesis. The allegory of the creation of "Manifest Man" is given in the second chapter. Together with these two allegories, there are four other important allegories and parables in the first eleven chapters of Genesis.

The other four that are important are "Adam and Eve" or the "Fall of Man"—which we are considering now, and which we are going to do fully. Then briefly we are going to do the others: "Cain and Abel"—we are going to sound out briefly. Then "Noah and The Ark." And finally the "Tower of Babel."

Now let us fully consider "Adam and Eve" or the "Fall of Man." The outer you is the Adam man. Has an intellect and has free will. Therefore, this intellect in you, with its free will, must decide for itself whether you will listen to the inner voice of Jehovah God—God individualized in you—to run your life. Or whether you will yield to the whimseys of outer man, and therefore not really grow—save through hard knocks.

Yielding to sense consciousness, the outer, has always produced the "Fall of Man." It did not just happen way back then. Every time you, who are so interested in Truth, come to a juncture in your life where there is a problem or a challenge; if, instead of your using the Truth, you just give in to the outer condition—you fall away from God.

The story of Adam and Eve begins with the fourth verse in the second chapter. Why? Because the first three verses of the second chapter actually belong in the first chapter. How did that happen? Well, at that time writers did not know much about paragraphs. Some still do not. But lack of knowledge, pertinent to paragraphs, accounts for the Bible's grammatical inconsistency here.

I am simply helping you to understand that the first three verses of the second chapter really are the last of the first chapter. So beginning with the fourth verse and continuing on in the second chapter, you have the story of Adam and Eve. It purports to tell you, by means of a parable, about yourself. It makes you to know that you are a composition of Adam and Eve. The two refer to your intellectual and emotional natures. Your intellect is symbolized by Adam, your emotional nature by Eve. It is not a case of there being literally a man and woman in a garden somewhere.

All people, then and now, have both the masculine and feminine in them. Did you know that? Has nothing to do with religion. It is a fact determined by science. That the parable here does the same, then, should not be so unusual. Adam symbolizes your intellect. Eve symbolizes your emotions. As the story goes, man's intellectual and emotional natures disobeyed Jehovah

God. Would not listen! So they were driven from the Garden of Eden.

Now the Garden of Eden is not some lovely spot in the Mesopotamia Valley. It is your eternal connection with omnipresent substance or the realm of divine ideas of God—its life substance or "know how" for your body, its love substance or "know how" for your human relations, and its prospering substance or "know how" for your supply and success. The Garden of Eden is your contact with all that. Yes, the contact to it is always right where you are!

This gives you a leverage over your challenges, if you have reached the point of using this substance. It allows you, through prayer, if something goes wrong with your body, to let in the substance or "know how" of God for the rehabilitation of the particular part. The same for your human relations. The same for your supply and success. It is like hooking a broken branch back to its tree. Then the sap of the tree flows into the branch once again.

Now we have the Garden of Eden straightened out as your eternal contact with the substance of

God. And now we have you straightened out as being both Adam and Eve, your intellectual and emotional natures. The parable goes on to say, that if you are smart, you will not eat of the "tree of good and evil." Why? Because it is this "good and evil" aspect of life that ensnares us.

You know what bothers the average student of the Bible? He reads this parable and knows it is important. But he cannot understand how this man, the finished product, having Elohim God, the Source behind him, and being the individualization of that, Jehovah God, could fall from that high estate by choosing to express something less. Another thing that puzzles the reader of the parable is that ALL men have fallen. The obvious answer, if you think it through, is that we were given only the POTENTIAL equipment in our beginning with God. We have to use it—to become it!

So the parable in the Bible is correct. You do have the equipment. You have the mental anatomy. You are the only one on this plane equipped for the conscious usage of God. But so many people do not like the word usage. They say, "If I must use that word in connection with

God, I prefer to say that God uses me." Well, I do not care how you phrase it. One may sound better than the other. But let us be honest about this point. If you have never yet used God or been used by Him, you have missed out on the larger portion of your being.

What do you think you are going to do—use Him up? Why do you think He created you? But to express Him! I do not care whether you say, "I let Him use me," or "I will use God." I AM CONCERNED whether you say, "I prefer to let God use me," but never actually experienced any kind of usage. Rather just go to church, pay your dues and have this nice little statement as some kind of aura around your head. The purpose of you, being in the spot you occupy, is to use God—however you want to phrase it. That is why you were created!

Now you are told here not to eat of the "tree of good and evil," and this is the key to the parable. Why did we all fall? And why do we continue to fall—until we get on to it. Notice it says the "tree of good and evil." It is this MIXED FRUIT that does the job on us. Listen to the words, "And the Lord commanded saying, Of every fruit of the garden thou mayest freely eat: But of the tree of the knowledge of good and evil, thou shalt not eat of it; for in the day that thou eatest thereof thou shalt surely die."

And, of course, you will remember in the parable that the serpent beguiled Eve. Who is Eve? Your feeling nature. And the serpent? Sense consciousness. So the serpent now says, "Ye shall NOT surely die." Implying God does not mean what He says. That we can break His law and not suffer the consequences.

Let me repeat, the key to the whole parable lies in the "tree of good and evil." If, where you are right now, there were something so evil that it could destroy your body in two or three weeks, you would not partake, would you? If there were something in this world so evil it could nullify all your earnings, all your income, lose your job for you immediately, you would not do it, would you? If there were something in the world so evil it could reduce your human relations immediately to tragic depths beyond anything you have ever known, you would not give yourself to it, would you?

But that would be a "tree of TOTAL evil."

Where we could see what must happen to us. That is not the point the parable is making. It says to watch out for the "tree of good and evil." Why? Because it implies something we can do and get away with, perhaps.

Let me get real personal. If you over-did a little bit for a couple of days, where would you break down first? I do not know. But you know. And you have a patent on it. You have had it a long time. It is your "tree of good and evil." Why? Because you conjure up good sensible reasons to yourself as to why you have it. Another person conjures up his special reasons why he has headaches. Still another conjures up his special reasons why he has sinus trouble. How long he has had it. Where he got it. And so forth. You see, we in our imagination invent our specialty of why we have a certain thing, and let the fact that we have had it a long time, compound it further. Some people say, "I've had it since I was nineteen. Worse now than it was then. My father had it. My grandfather had it. It's an heirloom." And there it is, you see. That is his "tree of good and evil."

Then in business, no one is going to do something that is totally evil. He would have to be out of his mind. But here we are in business, and we are at different levels of consciousness at different times. So at times we are in a slow period and there is lack, and so forth. But we are the first to explain it. How there happened to be this lack. That it was caused by the times. The company. The boss. Politics. Something else. We have it all "down pat." We have it all invented. We have it all explained to ourselves. In our imagination we invent good reasons. Or we take some fact out of the past—where we went through a low period—and we let it keep us low. We let ourselves be stuck with our scar. This is our "tree of good and evil."

In human relations, it is the same thing. We are not going to do something diabolical. But we have our peculiarities, you see. We invent our own specialty. We say such things as, "Yes, I feel that sort of way, but I'm that type." Which always amazes me. No further explanation is necessary, "I am what I am." That is the beginning and the end of it—as far as some people are concerned.

Then, while we are supposed to be expanding, we are always meeting someone who is on the perimeter of our lives. Does not go with our crowd. Is not our type. That is where we stop and get off. We have been getting off for years. We do not expand beyond that type and learn anything. We are stuck with that type. We are happy until we meet that type. We have invented our own specialty, "I'm a glorious creature as long as my type is around me. But I can't stand this type. And I can't stand that type. Deliver me from them." Yes, we have our own inventions. Good reasons why we remain in our limited human-relation environment. This is our "tree of good and evil."

So we allow our emotions (Eve) to rule us here. Function at the level of sensation (the serpent). Our Eve eats of that continually and she gives it to our intellect, then the two of us eat—both our feelings and our intellect. All of which brings us to that old adage which I dearly love. "If you do not react emotionally to your situation, you can win out." Yes, if you can be impersonal. See what you have been doing, and begin to change. Then you stop eating of your "tree of good and evil."

The whole essence of this parable is that the outer man of us must train himself to listen to his Real Self or Deeper Self. What we belong to in

God—in body, in business, in human relations. Rather than just respond emotionally to our senses—the serpent. Now if you capture the heart of the parable, you will always be on the lookout for the "tree of good and evil." Stop easing yourself down into your own rut. Begin to prepare yourself. Process yourself to eat of the "tree of life." Which is your total health, your total supply, your total order and happiness. Be on to it; eat of it—and expand!

"Cain and Abel" we said we would do briefly. Most of us remember certain lines of poetry since we were children. "Cain shot Abel in the neck with a brick," was one such line for me. I can remember it from the time I was eight or nine.

What do you know about the parable of "Cain and Abel?" Well it goes very simply. Cain was a man who worked for possessions only. Was extremely materialistic. Abel was inclined to spiritual ideas. And they both made offerings to Jehovah. Jehovah turned down Cain's offering. But accepted Abel's because it was given from a spiritual nature. Cain became angry and slew Abel. All of which means to you in this parable, how often do you let the material side of you slay

the spiritual? You know better. You have been a
Truth student for years. You know the way. The
path you should take. Yet you take the other. You
slay the spiritual. If you get the point of this
parable, you can be greatly helped.

A little later "Adam and Eve," who had given
birth to "Cain and Abel," were blessed with
another son. In the parable that son, named Seth,
symbolized compensation. Why? Because he,
too, was spiritually inclined. What is the key for
you? Stop letting the material side get in the way
of the spiritual side of you. Choose the spiritual
against just the material. But remember,
through this parable, that even though you
choose wrongly—"Truth crushed to earth will
rise again." It is not lost. The spiritual side of
you, that wants to become you, will keep coming back, saying, "Let me be in that side of your
life instead of denying me further." That is the
meaning of "Seth" in this particular parable.

Then "Noah and his ark" are extremely interesting. This is an allegory, you know. Possibly in
part taken from the myth of the Babylonians,
after the Jews' period of captivity under them.
Yes, the Jews may have accepted something of

this myth about a flood. Now the Babylonians believed in all kinds of gods in their Genesis, but they also made mention of a flood. The Hebrews believed in only one God in their Genesis, but they put a flood in their writings, too. I am not saying that there was no flood, but I explain by route of great scholars that there was this influence of a suggested flood—by the Babylonians.

So the story of Noah is told, and "Noah" represents something very special. He represents one who has found peace with God. Peace that comes from knowing he is protected—regardless of what the outer world goes through. This is the kind of man you want to think of yourself as being. For the Truth student does not have to wait for the world to wake up—to express the Truth. He does not have to go by the world.

Now the "Ark" in the allegory represents a positive state of consciousness. A positive saving state of consciousness. You must build this up. This consciousness is built when we rest in God and seek to do only His will. Not what the world is doing. The whole point here is that when evil conditions exist in the outer, they bring their own retribution. Such conditions need to be

redeemed before some great tragedy happens—
such as the flood in the allegory.

If we have prepared our "ark," we do not have
to fear the flood. The ark is something that every
Truth student has been gradually building up
through his study and his affirmations. Yes, you
are building up an ark of consciousness that is
saving you and protecting you from the times
through which you are passing.

The allegory offers this, too. It shows that this
spiritual man, "Noah," who symbolizes you in
the study of Truth, has an affection for all lower
forms of life. He wants to express spiritual dominion over them, so he brings into the ark these
lower forms of life for their perpetuation. This
kind of dominion is what God wants done
through you. Yes, treat all lower forms of life
with love.

The "bow in the sky," follows. It is part of the
healing when the flood is over. Always has had a
signal meaning. What God promises there—is an
answer to every cloud. This is the meaning of the
"bow." As an old adage has it, "Every cloud has a
silver lining." This is actually also a promise from
God.

The final allegory is the "Tower of Babel."
Some students of the Bible will insist that it is
pronounced "Bābel." But in its metaphysical
interpretation, it comes out "Bâbel" or (Babble).
You will see why. The descendents of Noah got
away from his spirituality. They became materialistic. That sometimes happens. So they decided
to build this tower high into the heavens. But
they had a wrong idea about it. They thought
that by material means they could make a
passageway unto heaven.

The point of the allegory is you cannot get into
the heaven of God through material means. You
cannot buy your way. You have to open yourself,
and really want it. These people got so lost in
material things, became so contrary to God's
laws—their speech was scattered. In other words,
they became confused. "Babble" reigned.

Just like today—you would be amazed how
many people are simply confused. They do not
know which way to go, which way to turn. They
have no rules or regulations. They follow this
fellow or that fellow. And one is as bad as the
next, you see. So they are all mixed up and
confused.

This confusion only happens when we do not listen from within. We are Truth students. Whatever the challenge, listen from within! Otherwise we, too, get lost in confusion—our tongues are scattered. But when we stay close to God, and take time to listen, we have the tongue that will calm any situation. And it is the tongue that is backed by the love of God. Your attitude or your way, then, regardless of the words you speak, will make its imprint. You will be all right, and those around you, the same.

Spiritual Meditation

Together with the allegory of "Creation in Mind Only" (Genesis I) and the allegory of the "Formation of Creation in The Manifest," (Genesis II) there are four additional parables and allegories, depicting great Truths about you —in the first eleven chapters of Genesis. The following are brief interpretations of the remaining allegories.

Adam (outer intellectual man) was created with free will and therefore must decide for himself whether he will listen to the inner prompting of Jehovah God, the individualized presence of God as Spiritual Man in him, or yield to the outer prompting of sense consciousness. Yielding to sense consciousness (the serpent) has always produced the "fall of man" or the falling away from God!

Thus the parable of "Adam and Eve" (man's intellectual and emotional natures) showed they disobeyed Jehovah God and were driven from the "Garden of Eden" (man's connection with omnipresent substance or the realm of all the divine ideas he could desire or need).

Eve gave Adam the forbidden fruit from the "tree of good and evil." All of which brings to mind the old adage, "If you do not react emotionally to a situation, you can win out"—Eve being the emotions.

"Cain and Abel" relate the overcoming of the spiritual nature in man temporarily by his carnal nature. "Seth" represents your spiritual nature rising again. "Noah and his Ark" represent a saving state of consciousness which complies with the Principle of Being in man. The "Tower of Babel" makes clear that you cannot reach heaven by material means. You only end with "babble" or confusion that way.

"Look unto Me, and be ye saved. . . ." Isaiah 45:22.

OLD TESTAMENT

PART IV.

"ABRAHAM, SARAH AND YOU"

"Lift up thine eyes, and look from the place where thou art, northward and southward, and eastward and westward: for all the land which thou seest, to thee will I give it."

Genesis 13:14,15
American Standard Version

"And the Lord said unto Abram, Get thee out of thy country, and from thy kindred, and from thy father's (human father) house, unto the land that I will show thee."

Genesis 12:1
American Standard Version

"And I will make of thee a great nation, and I will bless thee, and make thy name great."

Genesis 12:2
American Standard Version

"And Abram took Sarai his wife, and Lot his brother's son, and all their substance that they

68

had gathered, and the souls they had gotten in Haran; and they went forth to go into the land of Canaan, and into the land of Canaan they came."   Genesis 12:5
                            American Standard Version

In this segment of the Bible we are going to consider some tremendous material, which relates itself to our lives. This is the fourth highlight in the series on the Old Testament—"Abraham, Sarah and You." Since Abraham is the first literal man in the Bible authenticated with actual background, I thought we might have a brief review.

We have understood that the first eleven chapters of the Bible in Genesis are a combination of parables and allegories. And since the dictionary makes no great distinction between the two, I suggest that you accept them as approximately the same thing. Basically, that it is telling a story, either fictional in the parable, or pertaining to something factually familiar to everyone in the allegory. In either case telling the story for the express purpose of illustrating a great Truth and its relation to you.

With that understanding, we now see clearly that Genesis first gives us our perfect position in life. Elohim God as the Father everywhere equally present. Jehovah God as His individualized presence in man. Adam as the outer man with intellect and free will. And when Adam finally learns to do only the will of God, he is transformed into Jehovah God or his Real Self—having the same meaning as the term "Christ" in the New Testament.

Next, Genesis tells us what to do from that position. In other words, it gives us our Eternal Creative Process by means of its Seven Days of Creation.

Then Genesis tells, by means of the parable of Adam and Eve, how man fell from both his position and true creative process—through the misuse of his free will.

The parable continues with Cain and Abel, the children of Adam and Eve. Cain was more or less lost in material things. Abel was more interested in spiritual things. So the offerings that Cain gave back to God and the offerings that Abel gave back were different. The offerings of Abel were more readily received because he was more in tune with God. Jealous of this, Cain slew Abel, meaning the material side of us sometimes temporarily overcomes the spiritual side.

But Seth, a child like unto Abel, was born a little later to Adam and Eve, meaning that "Truth crushed to earth will rise again." In other words, the spiritual side of us will eventually triumph.

The son of Seth was Enoch, who according to the parable learned to walk completely with God. And he was translated. It is the story of a great Truth that if you learn to live totally with the will of God, you can be translated from this plane.

The son of Enoch was Methuselah. And he lived 969 years. The point for you is this. Enoch lived a very short time, yet he was translated because he did only the will of God. Methuselah lived 969 years. But that is about all that was recorded in his favor. Meaning what? That longevity is not necessarily the essence of living. It is pointing out that how much you do, not how long you live, is what counts.

Genesis continues by telling us the Story of Noah, The Ark and The Flood. The point of which is what? That if things in the outer world get bad enough due to the general wayward thinking of the race, a purge may be necessary such as symbolized by "the flood."

What I did not tell you before, but which I will include in this review is as follows: There were three sons of Noah. There was Ham, Shem and Japheth.

In the parable Ham was the physical one, Shem the spiritual, and Japheth the mental. The story makes very clear that Shem, the spiritual one, and Japheth, the mental one, worked closely together to keep Ham "in line." And this is the point the parable makes for you. The spiritual and the mental of you work closely together to keep the physical you in order—once you begin to give them the opportunity.

Genesis concludes its parables and allegories with the Story of The Tower of Babel. The people in the story built a tower high in the heavens on the theory that through material means they could find their way to heaven. That could never be. It was really a tower to self service. And self service, if that is your total method of living, leads to confusion. Confusion of tongues, such as is given in the story. Through the story you see that self service is not the answer to life. You have to serve others. Get the right Spirit. Become a tower of God yourself, into which those who have needs—"run and are safe," as the Bible puts it.

That is our thumb-nail sketch of the Bible to date. And it has been worth repeating in brief.

Now we come to the first literal person in the Bible, Abraham. Basically, it is the historical account of Abraham and Sarah. But as their life's story starts out—those were not their names. His name was Abram and hers, Sarai. However, both had their names changed during the course of their lives. Right now, though, I want to emphasize that Abraham was the first literal person in the Bible. There is no question about that. His background is authenticated. He was the first of the patriarchs of the Hebrews.

Now, let us get a graphic picture of Abraham. With the 12th chapter of Genesis, Hebrew history begins. The family of Abraham belonged to one of the Semitic tribes that migrated to the neighborhood of Ur in the south of Mesopotamia. That is the region from which his people came.

This is the authenticity of Abraham. This is what is known as pre-bible knowledge. His people were highly civilized people. They lived in well-planned cities. They worked in bronze. They used a potter's wheel. They had a very accurate system of weights and measures. They cultivated the science of astronomy—not astrology. Astronomy, an exact science, by which you can tell an eclipse to come one thousand years from now. But they cultivated astronomy with spiritual overtones. I mention all this to show that Abraham was a literal person.

Abraham was known as the father of the Hebrews. For it was under his leadership that his group separated itself from the other Semitic tribes and settled in Canaan.

Now today by connotation we think of Jewish people in terms of religion. And that is the way it should be. But here is their actual background. The Bible refers to the descendants of those that settled in Canaan as Hebrews, which was their racial name. Later on, Israelites became their religious name. The name, Jews, was given them about the time of the Babylonian captivity. All the Hebrews there in captivity at that time were from Judah, which was the half of their kingdom that was destroyed, the other half being Israel. Thus the name, Jew, obviously was derived from Judah. Interesting, is it not?

Their kinsmen in those days were the Babylonians, the Assyrians, the Armenians, and the Phoenicians. At one time or another they were under the captivity of all of these kinsmen.

All of this is a kind of a preface to our subject, "Abraham and You." This background is literal history. But we need to understand here that history, too, is just the "rack" upon which the "spiritual meat" is hung—the same as in an allegory or a parable. The thing that is important is to relate what counts to your own unfoldment.

Yes, relate what counts in the Bible to yourself, for the Bible boiled down is nothing more than the story of the involution and evolution of God's Spirit in man—involved in him and finally evolved through him. And you must read it from that context. It is this journey into light, which is the story of the Bible.

So when you read the Bible, always remember where you are reading in point of time. People's religious level of unfoldment at that time. Their superstitions at that time. Their morals at that time. Once you get on to this, and realize basically that what you are after are the keys to your life—seeing in and through these times what is needed or not needed by you—then you have the message the Bible offers.

Now here is made plain the relation of Abraham to you. Abraham, historically represents the first of the patriarchs of the Hebrew race. But metaphysically—something else. His early stage as Abram, before he reached his peak of faith, symbolizes the first step in the redemption of yourself from where you are. It does not imply full and complete faith on Abram's part—it was not. He was moving from here to there. He was growing through faith. He represents the beginning of faith toward a new land or new level of life—and that is where you are. You want a new land, a new experience in body, business and human relations—everything about your person. Well, that requires a new consciousness. The law is, "As within, so without." If you want to go into the new, it requires something new in you.

But the beginning of faith is the willingness to follow the guidance of God. And this is where we find Abram. He was willing to follow the guidance of God. Now if you are willing to follow the guidance of God, you are starting with Abram where he was. What does that do? This inspires you to go forth into a new land—or new consciousness.

If you take yourself seriously in Truth, you are always seeking the new land—the new consciousness. You should have a goal now. We progress by goals. We want to come out of some of the aches, pains and troubles we have in the body. Difficulties we have in human relations. Limitations we have in the financial world. We want to find more of the "life more abundant."

Being so inspired—and I believe that you are —you must be willing to leave the old states of mind that caused the difficulties.

I was talking to someone long distance recently and she has challenges in her body, in her human relatins, and in her finances. I talked to her as best I could over the phone, and she said, "I am not aware that I have any of these limitations in my subconscious at all." I said, "Well, I don't want to pick a fuss with you, but 'as within, so without.' If you've got a bad deal in your body, your human relations, and your finances, believe me, you have a little something to clean up in your subconscious." That is all I could tell her, you see. So if you do not like what is happening out here in your world, then you know there is a clean up needed within. And that is a wonderful beginning!

All right, now in this Abram state, which is just the beginning of faith, he is willing to accept God's guidance to a new level. There are two great Truths emphasized, which Abram willingly accepted, and the point is—are you?

First, God Himself wishes you to move into this new land. He wanted it before you felt it. The fact that you feel it now means you are ripe for this experience. But this new land requires entirely new viewpoints from God—about your body, your human relations, your finances and so forth.

Second, God actually wants to bless you in this experience. He wants you to arrive in the new land. He wants you to have it. He wants to give you a new name or a new nature. Put you on a higher level than you are now. Show forth the new good to which you aspire. He wants this to happen. He wants to bless you with it. The lack of not having it now—is not due to the divine intent of God. Rather to your own inability up 'til now to accept what He has prepared. You have accepted only so much good, you see. But "Eye hath not seen, nor ear heard . . ." the new things He has prepared for you.

Getting back to the historical account, Abram was joined now by his wife, Sarai, and his brother's son, Lot, for his journey to the new land of Canaan. Sarai was his wife's name at the outset, not Sarah as she was later renamed by God. The reason being Sarai was not fully unfolded at this point. She represented the feeling nature, only partially developed—not intuitional enough as yet. Lot, his brother's son, was obvious. He symbolized faith—but faith only in material things. Due to their limited natures, both Sarai and Lot influenced Abram wrongly!

So these were Abram's comrades. Lot had to prove a "drag," as they say in today's parlance, because his faith was only in material things. Sarai could not give Abram the benefit of intuition or God's guidance because she did not have it. She was not fully developed spiritually, just very dear and beautiful. Together, therefore, these comrades represented insufficient equipment to sustain Abram's faith. And he was just beginning in his faith and willingness to go with God's guidance into a new land.

Now that we have the picture. Stop for a minute and ask yourself this. In the past have you ever made a change—and had with you companions who were not fully developed—and were not too unfolded yourself? If so, you have to remember that this was all a part of your consciousness then. That it attracted theirs. You must not blame anyone. This is where you were. This is a good time to pause for a moment, think back—and learn.

Abram learned his lesson. First, though, Abram faltered because those with him did not sustain his faith. They did not have the unfoldment. So we are told that on his first attempt to enter Canaan and live there—a famine came. This caused Abram to do something. He went to Egypt.

"Egypt" represents sense consciousness to which we all are apt to retreat when things go awry. That is exactly what Abram did. You see, the Bible tells it the way it is. With him as with us, if things do not work out for us when attempting to rise to a new level by spiritual means, we are apt to revert back to the best way of living we knew on our former material level.

So Abram went down to Egypt with his companions, Lot and Sarai. He just let go of all his spiritual plans. Down there he became very material. He passed off his wife, Sarai, to the Pharaoh of Egypt as his sister. She was most beautiful, as you know. He passed her off as his sister to get all the help he could from the Pharaoh. The Pharaoh was quite taken with her, and fell in love. Abram naturally got all the benefits out of the affair, that he sought.

Then sooner or later, as it always does, the Truth came out that this was not his sister, but his wife. And what do you think happened? Pharaoh ordered him out of Egypt. In other words, sense consciousness would be rid of the spiritual that would not represent itself truly or go the whole way in faith. Have you ever noticed this? That people, who are very material, cannot stand someone who professes to be spiritual; but given the chance—is just as material as they are. They do not want such around. But if a person is truly spiritual, and depends upon it, even material people respect that. Such is what happened to Abram. But Abram learned his lesson. How does this help you? If you borrow from Abram's experience here. Learn from it. You do not have to go through the trouble here, he attracted to his person.

Abram learned his lesson, returned to Canaan and became rich, symbolizing his increased power of faith. This time he tackled it spiritually —his new land. He and Lot became so rich in flocks, that they hardly had land enough for them. Abram finally separated his flock from Lot's, enabling each man to go his separate way. He let Lot make a choice as to the part of the land he wanted, showing how spiritual Abram had become. Letting his brother's son have first choice, Lot chose the fertile plain around Sodom and Gomorrah, so his flocks could eat well. Abram took the rocky hills of Hebron. It looked like a bad bargain.

But something happened. God compensated Abram because of his great generosity here—causing him to lift up his eyes to see from the heights. So no matter what your situation may be now, the point here is, if you learn to see from the heights, lift up your eyes and see from the heights —God can prosper you however rocky your soil. Your blessing will be greater than that for which you could just humanly hope. Yes, look from where you are—southward, northward, eastward, westward—and really see God working with you and making your land fruitful.

This is what Abram did. And things went well for him. But Lot remained grossly selfish. Like anyone who lives his life only from the material, and becomes grossly selfish—negative things have a way of happening "hand over fist."

What happened to Lot was this. The neighboring tribes attacked Sodom and Gomorrah and overwhelmed the people. Lot's lands, herds and so forth were confiscated, and Abram had to come to his rescue. Abram gathered his men and rescued Lot and his family. This represents a great Truth, that when permitted, faith in the spiritual will always prove superior to faith in the material—in the long run.

While Lot and his wife and children escaped the destruction of Sodom and Gomorrah through Abram, Lot's wife did not benefit because she looked back and became a pillar of salt. Now someone reads that and says, "How ridiculous can the Bible get? Surely that did not happen." No. But the inner meaning of it did—that she was preserved in the past. The point for you is this: It symbolizes that when one is freed of a difficulty, as she was, it is disastrous to look back. Now just think for a minute what this means!

You have come out of a great difficulty, let us say, where you were all hemmed in. And, according to material forces, they were going to keep you there. Yet because you believed in God, somehow that was dissolved and you were lifted above them and placed in a whole new deal for yourself. Now if you look back and say, "Even though I was in prison then, it was more pleasant than it is now." That is dangerous. You have come to a new land. Give yourself to the new land. That is the point this episode is making!

Having gone through many episodes with our friend, Abram—seen ourselves in each and learned from each—we now approach the last. Abram and Sarai were childless, even though God promised a child out of the marriage. Abram tried to force the issue. He opened himself to the suggestion of Sarai, his wife, that he take unto himself her Egyptian handmaiden. Which he did, and through this person a child was born, known as Ishmael.

But it was not a satisfying working out. This was not the son of God's promise to Abram and Sarai. This episode symbolizes two Truths that you should learn—to rest in the Lord—and wait patiently for Him. Let me emphasize that. Out of the long years I have been in this field, the more mature I have become, the more I have learned to "rest in God's action and wait upon Him" to bring the thing to me. Oh, I will do all the outer steps that come to me to do, but there is a definite sense of resting and waiting on a Power greater than self to bring it about.

Now that is the main thing Abram had to learn in this lesson. The other thing was that if you try to force your good, that too is not satisfactory. He tried to force the circumstances by which a son could be born to him, using a handmaiden. Instead of waiting for the Lord to bring about the birth through Sarai.

Abram realized his mistake. Finally in his growing faith, he waited again upon the Lord's covenant—that a son would be born to himself and Sarai. Thus he allowed his insufficient faith to become sufficient faith, and the Lord changed his nature to one of sufficient faith. That is why the Lord changed his name to Abraham.

For the same reason the Lord changed Sarai's name. Remember, her feeling nature was not spiritually developed. But through all these experiences with Abram, having continued to open herself to spiritual growth, God changed her undeveloped feeling nature into one of great intuition. In keeping with the change in her nature, the Lord then changed her name from Sarai to Sarah.

Note that the changed natures in both Abraham and Sarah came first, then the changed names—not the other way around as some people superstitiously do.

Out of this dual change, the promised child, Isaac, was born, symbolizing joy. Proving that all God requires for answered prayer, or a joyous production in your life, is this wholehearted return to Him. Yes, through faith and intuition, believing, listening and taking the outer steps that come to you to do, then you shall reach the land you seek.

In closing, Abraham had some finishing touches to make with God to complete this particular journey he was taking with God. And in making them, he has some finishing pointers for you.

Abraham was told from within, "Go with the light of God." Yes, "Go out into the length and breadth of the land you see from your lifted vision, and I will give it to thee." But remember the giving is from within. Yes, if you give your faith and intuition to God, the giving is from within. The human may say, "I am too old." "The odds are too much against me." "It's too late now." Or whatever. But God, if you are listening, says: Put yourself in the role of him that hath the new health—hath the new supply—hath the new order in his life. Put yourself psychically or mentally in the role that you would like to play.

Then the decision will come from within. The conviction will be born. The timid, old self will go. And you will experience a new self of greater dimension than you have known. That self will possess the new land. The new goal that you have in mind!

This is true action and reaction, working with God. Act correctly from within concerning anything out here. Toward this new land you want to possess, for example. And you will find yourself reacting properly out here in due season. You finally will know that you are going to enter into your new goal.

Boiled down it amounts to assuming something from God. Having faith in Him. Having a willingness to listen. Having the feeling that you are going to reach your next goal.

Yes, continue to proceed from this assumption. Proceed from within, putting yourself again and again in the role that you would like to play in your new land. Free others into this same Truth. Those who seemingly have been holding you back. Bless them and see them co-operating. And you will walk the length and the breadth of a bright new land—even as Abraham did!

Spiritual Meditation

We are glad for the illumination afforded by Truth. When it first comes to us, we feel like new creatures and are eager to enter the new land.

But we are required FIRST to surrender the error habits we have acquired, which are adverse to our spiritual nature. Yes, discard every human reason you have picked up which would keep you in your old land. Such as the peculiar reasons you have for your body weaknesses, lack of income, failure to succeed—your prejudices, resentments and resistance to your good. You cannot loiter there. Having heard the call with the Abram faculty of faith, go forward you must!

Then, SECOND, we are required to take on this realization following the quickening of our faith: That God has blessings in store for us. Yes, "I will bless thee, and make thy name great; and be thou a blessing." God wishes to give you great new good in the land that lies ahead—the land He bids you to enter. Your present lack of good, in any form, is not due to His divine intent; but to your inability to accept what He has prepared. Thus to enter the new land is contingent upon entering a higher state of consciousness to match the new land. As you prepare yourself and receive these new blessings, you give more of yourself to life and thus become a greater blessing to others.

"Get thee out of thy country" (present land or limited state of consciousness).

Amer. Std., Genesis 12:1

OLD TESTAMENT

PART V.

"JACOB, ESAU, ISRAEL AND YOU"

"And Esau said to Jacob, Feed me, I pray thee
. . . for I am faint: . . ."

> Genesis 25:30
> (King James Ver.)

"And Jacob said, Sell me this day thy birthright."   Genesis 25:31
> (King James Ver.)

"And He (God) said unto him (Jacob), What's
thy name? And he said, Jacob."

> Genesis 32:27
> (Amer. Std. Ver.)

"And He (God), again speaking to Jacob, said,
Thy name shall be called no more Jacob, but
Israel: for thou hast striven with God and with
men, and hast prevailed . . . and He blessed him
there."   Genesis 32:29
> (Amer. Std. Ver.)

91

We will consider in this subject one of the most unique sections of the Bible, the title being, "Jacob, Esau, Israel And You." But let us for a moment very briefly review where we have been as yet in the Bible.

We have considered in its original language the narrative of Genesis as to our beginning, and found the most exacting position for ourselves in life. We have, through the first eleven chapters of Genesis, considered Adam and Eve as a parable. We have considered, following Adam and Eve, the parables and allegories of the sons of Adam and Eve, their offspring Cain, Abel and Seth, plus Noah and the Ark and his sons, and the Tower of Babel. Last, we considered the first literal man in the Bible, Abraham, whose background has been verified as coming from a highly cultivated race of people. And we found much help for our faith through his life.

May I remind you, as we begin, that you must own the key to the Bible. Without it you read in vain. The key to the Bible, whether it is written in the terms of a parable, an allegory, or an historical event, is its relation to you. That is what the book is all about. It is the story of the involution of

God's Spirit into man, and its evolutoin into form through man. It is a gradual process. And every event, every character, every story has great meaning to your life.

At the beginning of this segment, we are going to consider Isaac as the second literal man among the patriarchs of the Bible. Abraham was the father of the Hebrew race and thus the first of the patriarchs. Isaac was the beneficiary of the results of Abraham's unfoldment.

Isaac typifies the person who was born into this plane with a healthy body, rich parents and lovely human relations—by reason of an un-folded, carried-over consciousness that attracted the "life more abundant." So we have here one of the loveliest stories in the Old Testament. It is the romance of Isaac and Rebekah. The happy Isaac consciousness claims its counterpart in Rebekah, who is described as the soul's natural delight in beauty. Apart from the good body, fine financial background and happy human-relations, Isaac wound up with a delightful com-panion for life. It is a beautiful story, an histori-cal story, but it also has a significant relation to you—especially the sons in the story.

Out of the union of Isaac and Rebekah, sons were born, namely Esau first and then Jacob. As Esau was born first, in keeping with the laws of that day, he was the direct heir of Isaac. Isaac's legacy to his first born was more than property and power. It contained also a carried-over spiritual covenant that God had made with Abraham, if you remember: "Lift up thine eyes, and look from the place where thou art, northward, and southward, and eastward, and westward: for all the land which thou seest, to thee will I give it, and to thy seed forever." (Amer. Std. Ver. —Genesis 13:14,15) What was given to Abraham was reaffirmed to Isaac. To bring about its fulfillment was a spiritual obligation with this family.

Now Esau was the first born, and he symbolizes the physical or that which we are first aware of in our early youth. Thus he could comprehend and appreciate the material value of the legacy, the property and power, but not necessarily the spiritual. Why? Because he operated largely from the physical level. Jacob, on the other hand, represents the mental side of us, which is a step up in evolution and nearer the spiritual. Eventually the mental side of us takes precedence over the physical side of us, of which we were first aware.

Esau was a very hairy man—that does not necessarily make him physical—but his actions and all showed this. By like token, Jacob's actions showed him to be largely a mental person. Jacob, therefore, could perceive the spiritual significance of the legacy, quite apart from the property and the power. Thus he was better equipped to carry it on as a spiritual mission. However, even though he was equipped to do that, he was not above coveting the material value of the legacy, which automatically would go to Esau, the first born.

In advance, I want to make it very clear that without question this is one of the funniest stories in the entire Bible. It is funny without anybody telling a joke. Because human nature, by itself, is simply a riot. If you can stand off and look at it, and watch what it does, it will really develop your sense of humor. Here we see that the mental phase of man's consciousness is closer to the spiritual than the physical. But leans to trickery on its own to obtain its ends, until it is fully spiritualized.

Let us capsule this story for ourselves in a way that will give us something to think about. Eventually the man, Jacob, becomes spiritualized and his name is changed to Israel. So here you have in this literal story, which happened in history, a portrayal of the three levels of man—the physical level, the mental level and the spiritual level.

It might be good at the outset of this juncture to ask yourself how much of you is still just physical? For example: Do you eat to live, or do you live to eat? If you live to eat, you are still physical. Do your appetites control you or do you control your appetites—in all directions? If your appetites control you, you are still physical. If you mean well in life, but like pleasure so much that pleasure comes first instead of whatever you should be doing, you are still physical. We all should have a rational amount of pleasure, but not to the point where it dominates our lives.

When you are very young, you are greatly concerned with the handsomeness of the man or the beauty of the lady. As you get older it is more "beauty is as beauty does." You become more mature. You evaluate life differently. As this lesson goes on—ask yourself how much of you is still mental—and only mental. Machiavelli, an infamous man in history, was noted for his pronouncements of spirituality, but you always found him reverting to his mentality when it came to expediting something. You know, he never let his spirituality stand in his way.

This, too, is a good question to ask yourself. How much of you as yet has become spiritual? How much of your reactions to life are spiritual —without thinking? Do you revert to God in each instance or are you lost in the world? These are things to ask ourselves as we get into this section. For, though this story actually happened, even history in the Bible is merely the "rack" upon which is hung the "spiritual meat."

As this story opens it touches your "funny-bone." Jacob plays upon the physical weakness of Esau in a strange way. Esau was out in the fields, and there was plenty of land that belonged to the family. He was a long way out, and the time came to eat. He was not satisfied much with what he had brought along. Jacob, on the other hand, having made a point of following Esau, brought with him some fine venison. And in the vicinity of our friend, Esau, cooked up a nice pot of porridge, with good venison in it. The aroma floated around, you know, and Esau was about to have some, because it was a lot better than what he had brought along.

Jacob in effect said, "Well, that's just fine. I've brought enough for two. Delighted to have your company. Join me, if you will." Except there was a little catch. By this time the saliva was well activated in Esau's mouth and he was ready to eat ravenously. To do anything to satisfy his appetite. It was suggested that he give away his birthright as the first born, to Jacob, who was next in line. And, if he would be so kind as to offer that little favor, Jacob in turn would be glad to give him all of the venison. Esau did not have to take any time to think. He was all for the venison. So he ate the porridge with the venison, and gave away his birthright as the first born, for the privilege.

Now you may say, "Well, he was kind of stupid." All right, then ask yourself about your own person physically. How often do you eat something or drink something that you do not need, but from which you derive a certain amount of pleasure—even though you know it is going to put on weight or injure your body? You see, this is life, is it not? How many times have you found yourself with something you should be doing, and you have said, "I'll put it off 'til tomorrow and enjoy today." Nobody reading this book, of course, but you might know someone who does. That is the physical man. He is controlled by his physical appetites.

But Esau had his own system of doing things. Although he gave away his birthright, the ease with which he gave it away was the same ease with which he took it back. He really did not mean it. So Jacob said to himself, "Well, I've got to figure out something more definite, because this fellow's word is worth nothing. He said, 'Yes,' yesterday but now he says, 'No,' keeping a tight hold on his birthright."

Jacob had a little helpmate in Rebekah, his mother. He was her favorite, instead of Esau. She thought Jacob was best equipped to carry on the family fortunes. So she helped him a little bit— by making him a pair of kid gloves. Not the kid gloves you wear today. They were made out of goatskin with hair on them. She told Jacob to put these on, you see, at that time when Isaac was reaching the point of making his transition. The custom was to call in one's oldest son for the blessing. It was an oral blessing. The father blessed the oldest son that everyone would know this is the one to carry on the family fortune.

Rebekah said in effect, "We'll prepare these

kid gloves for you, so when that time comes, we'll
have Esau out in the field somewhere, where he
likes to be anyway. You just get here, put on these
hairy gloves and sit by your father's bedside.
Isaac's vision is almost gone now, and he won't
know the difference. He'll just try to feel who it
is. He'll feel your arms and think—that for sure is
Esau. Why? Because there will be lots of hair on
your arms."

So that is what they did, Jacob and his mother,
Rebekah. They contrived to get the family
fortune for Jacob. And sure enough, Isaac felt the
arms and said, "Your arms feel like Esau but your
voice is a little more like Jacob." But he complied
and gave Jacob the blessing. Now Jacob was
legally the son who received the fortune. This
kind of thing does not go on any more, but such
was the way it was done in those days.

But Esau, as I said before, had a marvelous
ease of life. Nothing struck him with any finality.
When he heard that this trick had been played
upon him, he just got angry and gave every indi-
cation that he might commit mayhem on Jacob.

So Rebekah suggested strongly, and got permission from Isaac, that Jacob go back to Mesopotamia, the original homeland of Abraham. There to find a mate. Instead of taking a wife from Canaan, where they were, Jacob was to go back to the old lands, and get a wife there.

So off our friend, Jacob, goes. But his main purpose is really to get away from Esau, who took a dim view of the trickery involved. As Jacob goes on his way, he stops at Bethel. Remember, he is like the mental you, superior to the physical, but not above trickery. As yet he is not fully unfolded spiritually. The mental you is nearer to the spiritual than the physical you, but still has a few tricks in it. Nobody reading this, of course. But you know how this is with most everyone else.

Thus our friend, Jacob, has to grow, and he stops at Bethel. There he dreams that famous dream—called "Jacob's Ladder." In his sleep he sees angels ascending and descending on it. This is a very literal picture of prayer, and it adds to his consciousness. This is the beginning of spiritual growth for Jacob, who has been almost totally mental and full of tricks. The relation to you in this ladder to God is that each rung of the ladder is a layer of your consciousness going up in response to God. Going more deeply within is what is meant by "up." As it completes its response layer by layer, or rung by rung, it comes back "down," meaning outward again, ladened with the substance or "know how" of God for body, human relations, business or whatever. This is a true interpretation of prayer, and how it lets the outer you become one with what the Spiritual Self of you wants done.

The dream impressed our friend, Jacob. It was the beginning of a change in him to the spiritual through prayer. He had a long way to go. Some people study Truth for many years, and never get around to definite periods of spiritual treatment. You can listen to Truth and read Truth; but when you bring it down to prayer about your challenge, you are using it in treatment form.

From Bethel, Jacob continues on to Haran. There Rebekah's brother, Laban, has a lovely, beautiful daughter, named Rachel. Jacob falls in love with her, and she with him. All of which brings Laban into the picture as Jacob's possible father in law. Incidentally, Laban also proved to be the mental type, which you shall soon see. Jacob goes to Laban about the possible marriage. In those days the husband-to-be paid a dowry. If he had the money, fine—if not, he worked it out. Having asked Laban what arrangements could be made, Laban said in effect, "That's easy, just seven years of hard labor—service to me." And Jacob's love was so fervent, the Bible tells us, "that the seven years passed like seven days."

The marriage ceremony was arranged. But Laban had a problem that all fathers do—who have a number of daughters. It was necessary to get them all married. Having another daughter, who was as homely as Rachel was beautiful, there were no offers in her direction. And so—I warned you Laban was mental— Laban sent Leah into the bridal bed with Jacob, under cover of darkness, that he would mistake her for Rachel and thus accept the wrong daughter in marriage—as the Bible bluntly puts it in keeping with the crude marriage ceremony of those ancient days. Or you can use your imagination and put it more delicately—by saying Laban arranged the marriage ceremony supposedly of Jacob and Rachel in great detail and most deceptively. You can get the picture with me from a modern marriage ceremony. She is beautifully gowned, but with a veil over her face. When the ceremony is completed, Jacob leans over to kiss the bride. Naturally he lifts the veil, and—lo and behold—it is Leah instead of Rachel. He has married the wrong girl!

This does not bother Laban at all. He explains easily to Jacob, that a father has to take care of all his daughters, so there is no real loss. Jacob says in effect, "What do you mean, there's no loss. I have the wrong girl." And Laban says, "It's not as bad as all that. You can still have Rachel. All you have to do is work seven more years." There was not much Jacob could do about it, so he worked out the next seven years—and at long last got Rachel in marriage.

Jacob was a good worker, and he brought great prosperity to Laban. And you know, when you have a worker, who brings prosperity into the company, you do not like to let go of him. So Laban stayed up nights figuring out ways to keep him. And he kept him for another six years— twenty years having now passed. Finally, Jacob thought it was time to be on his way. He had more than prospered everybody concerned, and done his part nobly.

So he proposed to Laban that having done well by him, he would like to be on his way. Laban could not hold him any more, and they reached a kind of a bargaining stage. Jacob said that he would take the ringstriped, the speckled and the spotted cattle as his share for his twenty years of work. Then start his own life somewhere else. Laban agreed to that. But the occasion for this selection was sometime off. In the meantime Laban had his sons remove all the ringstriped, the speckled and the spotted cattle—so that it would be unlikely for them to bear any ringstriped, speckled or spotted offspring.

On discovering this, Jacob took a very dim view of it. That would not leave him many cattle. So he did not make his selection yet. He had an idea, too. Do you know what is going on here? When you are mental and full of tricks, life is strange about its hell for you. It is like a glove finely fitted to your hand. It may not have anything to do with the one whom you played tricks on, but your consciousness attracts to you—still another who is equally capable of playing similar tricks on you. That is consciousness. That is the way life is lived. Rarely is it the one to whom you have done it. But someone quite apart, who will do it unto you.

So Laban was just as mental as Jacob. They were a fair match. But Jacob was not whipped yet. He figured out a way he could still get the cattle. You know what he did? He got some poplar branches, some planter trees and some almond trees. All had dark bark. Cut the bark here and there, you know, and it is light underneath—making spots. So he put these cut-branches into the water trough where the cattle would drink. Knowing what? That when the cattle came to drink, they would naturally see all these spots before their eyes. Thus, in turn, they would conceive mostly of ringstriped, speckled and spotted offspring.

Now I did not make this up. That is the way it is told in the Bible. The point that it makes for you is this: That, what you focus your attention on largely in life, is what you draw unto yourself. That, whatever you give your attention to substantially, is what you attract. And it is a free world. The choice is yours. Successful people learn to focus their attention on that which makes for the "life more abundant." Unsuccessful people—on that which makes for misery!

Well, finally our friend, Jacob, wins out

through this method of hypnotizing the cattle to produce the kind he wanted—and he is on his way. But his wife, Rachel, makes a tiny mistake. She takes some of the "images" with her, or gods. Now this is a One-God community, you understand, but it has its relics of the past. Its people had these little images, which they kept in their houses. They did not necessarily worship them any more; but they were symbols of the past, and they were rather expensive.

Laban thought that was a marvelous reason for going after Jacob and his entourage—and bringing them back. It took him a while to catch up with Jacob. But he did not prove his case, because Rachel was the thief, his daughter of whom he was most fond. She was with child, and she was seated on a covering which hid the images. This was her arrangement in the tent, when Laban and his group arrived. She excused herself from getting up because she was with child, but really because the images were under her. She got away with it. It seems she had picked up a bit of the chicanery practiced by her husband, Jacob, and her father, Laban.

Now Jacob and his party were on their

way back to Canaan. And Jacob realizes that he has a brother there, whom he did not leave behind—with the greatest rapport. He wondered, after twenty years—was Esau still harboring a grudge? He then heard "via the grapevine" that more than harboring a grudge, Esau was bringing 400 people with him to meet Jacob. And Jacob said to himself in effect, "This man is not very forgiving."

So Jacob prayed about this. But he was still quite mental and capable of tricks. So he decides to send waves of his people ahead with gifts. The first wave may not make a dent, but the second and third and fourth with gifts—might warm Esau up considerably. The purpose being, that when Jacob got there, it would be a happy reunion.

Now that was a pretty good trick, but Jacob is growing spiritually. And while he is still up to his old tricks, he finally reaches to God and totally seeks to let God's will be done in this matter. He decides to pray all night about it. Realizing: "One is greater than I. God may be individualized in me, but I am not fully His will or way as yet. However, I am open with all my heart." So he prayed all night. We are told that he wrestled with a "Man"—not an angel—but a Man. The Man here is your Deeper Self, this individualized Self of God within you. Jacob is praying that he might become more spiritual. Have a different kind of consciousness. He tells the Man with whom he is wrestling, that he will not let go of Him unless given a blessing.

In the course of the scuffling, Jacob was smote on the underside of his thigh. To this day, the people who revere that particular episode, have meant well, but have picked the wrong thing to treasure. They do not eat the meat under the thigh. That became the custom. You see, you can get lost in customs and miss the real point. The main thing was that here was Jacob wrestling with his Real Self—as all of us should be taught to do. He repaired to that, opened himself and got his blessing. A change, a transformation, that only God can do—was wrought in Jacob. It was then a happy reunion with his brother, because he had attained his Real Self. Thus he came off at his best. Interesting, is it not?

This Man, this Spiritual Self or Jehovah God, had asked our friend, Jacob, "What is your name?" And he said, "Jacob." Then the Man, the Real Self, said, ". . . thy name shall be called no more Jacob, but Israel. . . ." (Amer. Std. Ver.— Genesis 32:29) And "Israel" was now the outer man of Jacob, who had made at one ment with God, and had become spiritual. Israel was an earlier name for the Christ, just as Jehovah God was an earlier name for the Christ, the individualized Presence of God in man. And frankly, everyone is an Israelite today, who believes in the One God and who seeks to take on spirituality from this individualized Presence within himself.

Now that is a great story, is it not? You see the physical man, and how limited he is. You see the mental man, who takes precedence over him. Everybody "ogles" this type, says he is so great, yet he is full of tricks. He has a long way to go, too. Finally, you behold the Spiritual Man. So we have witnessed Esau the physical, Jacob the mental, and Israel the spiritual!

Ask yourself, if you have digested this historical story? After all it actually happened. How much of the physical, Esau, do you still have in you? How much of the mental, Jacob, do you still have in you, who like Machiavelli purports great spirituality, but when it comes to expediting something reverts to mental tricks? And how much of the spiritual, Israel, have you become? How much has been allowed to rise to the surface and become you at this stage in your spiritual ongoing? IF YOU DO NOT CARE, NOTHING HAPPENS. IF YOU DO—GREAT CHANGES CAN TAKE PLACE IN YOU!

Spiritual Meditation

One of the loveliest stories in the Old Testament is the romance of Abraham's son, Isaac, with Rebekah. The happy Isaac consciousness claimed its counterpart in Rebekah, ". . . the soul's natural delight and beauty." Of this union sons were born, Esau and Jacob. As Esau was born first, he was the direct heir of Isaac.

All of which brings us to another story. If you are open, here in this chapter you can find the meaning of your life, from its lowest to highest level.

"Esau" represents the physical man and the fact that man is first aware of himself as a physical being. How much of "Esau" do you still have in you? Where your physical appetites so control you as yet, that you would sell your divine birth-right for a "mess of pottage" due to the false satis-faction of the moment.

"Jacob" symbolizes the mental phase of man's consciousness, which is closer to the spiritual than the physical, but leans to trickery. How much "Machiavelli," the Italian nobleman so like Jacob and famous for professing high spiritual principles but always acting according to expediency—is still in you?

"Israel" means the final Spiritual Man you are intended to become. How much of "Israel" has been attained by you through saying to each challenge, "Wist ye not I must be about my Father's business?" and then turning to God through prayer in faith believing?

"For thou hast striven with God and with men and hast prevailed. . . ."

Amer. Std., Genesis 32:29

OLD TESTAMENT

PART VI.

"JOSEPH, MOSES AND YOU"

"And the daughter of Pharaoh came down to wash herself at the river . . . and when she saw the ark . . . she sent her maid to fetch it. And Pharaoh's daughter said . . . Take this child away, and nurse it for me . . . and the child grew . . . and was brought . . . unto the Pharaoh's daughter, and he became her son."

Exodus 2:5,9,10

(King James Version)

"Now Moses kept the flock of Jethro his father in law, the priest of Midian: . . ."

Exodus 3:1

(King James Version)

"And God said unto Moses, I AM THAT I AM: and he said, Thus shalt thou say unto the children of Israel, I AM hath sent me unto you." ". . . the Lord God of Abraham, the God of Isaac, and the God of Jacob, hath sent me unto you: this is My Name forever, and this is My memorial unto all generations."

> Exodus 3:14,15
> (King James Version)

"And the whole congregation of the children of Israel murmured against Moses and Aaron in the wilderness."

> Exodus 16:2
> (King James Version)

Our subject is "Joseph, Moses and You." It is the sixth highlight of the Old Testament preparatory to the New Testament—which could not have been without that which we now consider.

In our spiritual prayers, and through them our spiritual progress, you and I have to pass through many experiences. Such marks the time our faith was first quickened until we come into a comprehension of the word "Lord." Then we are on a solid footing for our spiritual advancement. To most people, the word is simply another term for God, which is all right; but to the more advanced —its fuller meaning is that of the Higher Law of God. Much later, Jesus personalized Higher Law and thus was also called the Lord. This is a tremendous goal for all of us. Moses commemorates it for us, and by the time this segment is finished, I trust your consciousness will be laid upon the foundation of the Laws of God. Then you will have an entirely new view of yourself as you go forth in Truth.

Now the lives of Abraham, Isaac, Jacob and Joseph were actually typical of some of the experiences through which all of us pass, ere we stand firm in the understanding of Higher Law as the foundation of our lives. You see, the Law was not revealed, this Higher Law of God—to Abraham. His sustaining power was faith, and we really appreciate that. He started out with his helpful background of the One-God understanding. But his sustaining power was only from faith, without the added knowledge that God operates by Law.

So before faith can become full, come into its full power in your life, it must have as its foundation an understanding of God as Law, as the Higher Law of your being. This is brought home to us by Moses. And this is what we must learn from this chapter.

We perceived during the patriarchial period, the patriarchs of the Hebrew race, Abraham, Isaac, Jacob and Joseph—that man was what? Going forward steadily. We saw this advancement through each patriarch. There were some lapses, to be sure, but the graph was definitely upward. There was no great dilemma.

Now we are going to consider a change in that. It might be termed the "big slump." It is depicted by the enslavement of the Israelites in Egypt. Proving what? That faith without understanding God as Higher Law is insufficient. Confronted with such a great slump, faith deteriorates to the sense level and becomes the servant of worldly pride, power and greed—represented by Egypt.

Let us get behind this story, for a moment. Let us talk about you and me. We are all growing up. In our Truth, like Abraham, we have lived with faith. We have believed we have found great faith. But suppose we had hit something quite rugged and our faith did not let through the Higher Action we needed. If you are honest with yourself, you can see yourself here in this historical story. For a while your faith became the servant of the world again—its pride, power and greed. What everybody else did, you did. Sort of saying to yourself, "Well, I tried and didn't make it, so I will return to whatever the rest do." Does that strike a recognizable note in you. But it is not the end of your experiences.

It is like someone in Truth who said, "I reached a point where I threw all my books out the window." You may say, "He is not telling me anything new. But here I will tell him something new. He will go out that window and get those books back!" Is that not so? I have merely cited an experience many Truth students go through.

Now you may be asking yourself, "How in the world did the Israelites get back down into Egypt from Canaan?" We had Jacob, you will remember, coming back to Canaan as a spiritual man— his name changed to Israel. Meeting Esau, whom he had done a bad turn in the past, but with whom he now had squared himself. This was Canaan, and they were all back together. How, then, did this good race now called Israelites get back down into Egypt and into such troubles?

Well, to explain, I am going to do something very quickly, because reviewing Moses' life is our goal. But briefly we are going to consider Joseph, who followed Jacob in line of importance in the Old Testament.

Joseph represents expanding faculties in man through his study of Truth. He is broadening; he is growing. In particular, Joseph represents imagination, which is a tremendous faculty, and which needs to be wakened in all of us. Also, he represents the ability to interpret dreams. Today that is not so popular. We are more prone to get our guidance directly through prayer rather than through dreams, which is an indirect way. But it is still a valid way. My mother was great with dreams. Especially recurrent dreams and their interpretations. Seemingly she received much help out of that. Most people today may dream, but they do not even remember them. The ones they do remember are usually from hamburgers with onions late at night, or something like that. However, occasionally you have someone with recurrent dreams, who can tell you all the details. This is God reaching us indirectly to guide us. Indirectly—because the symbols in the dream must then be interpreted, as Joseph did.

But speaking from one who wrote a book on dreams—a great, great soul with whom I was privileged sort of to grow up. He said this about dream books, "They use certain standard images that most people may dream about, and through them they interpret the dream. You know, a cow means this, a tree symbolizes this, and lightning in the sky means something else. These can be helpful. But as a writer of a dream book myself," he said, "I would have to tell you that the best way to interpret your dream is to go back to the One who gave it to you in the first place— God. He will give you the best answer to the dream that is recurrent, if through prayer you sincerely ask for the correct interpretation." Interesting answer, is it not? This, mind you, from the author of a dream book.

So Joseph stood out as a developer of imagination and as an interpreter of dreams. He was the favorite son of Jacob—to place him in the history of your Bible. He was the firstborn of Rachel, Jacob's beloved wife. Benjamin was a brother, the only brother born through Rachel, also. Then there were six half brothers born through Leah, the first wife of Jacob. Two more by Rachel through her hand-maiden, and two more by Leah through her hand maiden, making twelve in all. Why do I take time to mention this? Here we have the beginning of the twelve tribes of

Israel through these twelve sons. But Jacob's favorite was Joseph.

Now let us briefly consider Joseph because he is the link between Jacob and Moses. Jacob loved him so much he gave him a coat of many colors. You all know that from your Sunday School days. This did not make him stand in too well with his brothers, since he was already the favorite of Jacob. You know, to get a coat of many colors, I do not know what that would be comparable to today, but it would stand out. Anyway his brothers took a dim view of it. And Joseph did not help matters. Because he not only interpreted dreams, but also dreamed dreams—that played himself up.

He told his brothers that he had this dream where one shaft of wheat stood up and the other eleven shafts of wheat bowed down to it. It did not take them long to figure out who the other eleven were. Then Joseph compounded the felony by telling his father and mother and eleven brothers about another dream—in which the sun and the moon and eleven stars bowed down to him.

What does all that mean? Well, Joseph, being an expanding person with imagination and so forth, and being very young, was using his imagination for his own vain glory. I do not have to tell you that it got him into more trouble. The brothers would not put up with him. They soon threw him into a pit—out in the field, you will remember. Then they killed a lamb, spilled the blood on Joseph's beautiful coat of many colors, and took it back to Jacob—saying that he was destroyed by an animal. Then they sold Joseph to a passing caravan that was travelling to Egypt. In other words, they got rid of him. That is the long and short of it.

Now Joseph is down in Egypt. That is the beginning of the Exodus of the Israelites from Canaan into Egypt, led by our friend, Joseph. He works for Potiphar in his enslavement. Potiphar is a fine man, captain of the Pharaoh's guards. But his wife takes a liking for Joseph and makes advances, with Joseph repudiating all such advances. Finally, in one of these struggles, she got a part of his shirt. She uses that to indicate Joseph made advances to her. Thus, Potiphar's wife had him thrown into prison.

In prison he had an interesting time. Because the prisoners did that which no one could stop them from doing, even in prison. And that was to dream a lot. So there with him in prison was this chief of the butlers and this chief of the bakers to the Pharaoh—both in disfavor. Our friend, Joseph, interpreted their dreams for them. For the butler, it got him back into his position as chief butler again. But in interpreting the dream of the chief baker, he was told that in three days he was going to be doomed—and that is the way it worked out. The butler got back into the Pharaoh's good graces—the baker obviously did not.

Joseph hoped that the butler would remember him, and speak a good word to the Pharaoh. But he forgot all about Joseph. However, Pharaoh, in time, dreamed a recurrent dream. The first dream was that cattle came up from the river Nile and were fat and well fed. But they were followed by cattle that came up from the Nile and were skinny and impoverished—and they ate the fatted cattle. The second dream was that corn appeared on this particular stalk. It was plentiful, beautiful, wholesome and enriching. Then corn appeared on the stalk which was impoverished looking—and it ate up the good corn.

Pharaoh could find no one able to interpret these recurrent dreams.

The butler finally remembered Joseph, and told Pharaoh about him. So Pharaoh sent for Joesph. Joseph came and told him that the dreams meant there would be seven years of plenty followed by seven lean years. The essence of it was this: (Babson of the Babson Institute got his idea from it.) That whenever you have inflation—we, of course, never bother with things like that in our time—but whenever you have inflation a recession has to follow of equal size and of equal density. That is the finding of the Babson Institute, which may or may not be accurate. But at least, so we are told. I would suggest you pray about that.

This is how important the Bible is with its material. And what happened? The Pharaoh made Joseph second in command of the whole of Egypt. Save for royal degrees, he was the big man. He brought his brothers down from Canaan because there was a famine there. He was not too easy with them. He let them work out a little something first, before he forgave them—using Benjamin. But that is another story. The main thing here was, he did forgive them. The thing I remember most from it was, "You meant it for my harm"—what his brothers had done—"but God meant it for my good." Does that mean something to you? Something somebody has done to you—meant for your evil—but as you look back on it now, God still turned it into good.

So the famine brought the family down to Egypt from Canaan. Then, Joseph, through the Pharaoh, set them up in the northeastern part of Egypt—Goshen—in the land of the Nile, where they remained for years. Beginning with Jacob's heirs, others followed. There they multiplied, became very rich, and lived off the cream of the land. Until what? Until there came a Pharaoh who never heard of Joseph. And this Pharaoh turned the tables completely. Made the Israelites slaves. Took away all their wealth. Put them at the bottom of the "totem pole"—just the reverse. That is where they are in our story now.

The new Pharaoh decreed that all male children of this ever-increasing race of people—the Israelites—be killed. Yes, to cut down on them, even though they were slaves. And, at the time of that decree, Moses was born. He brought faith in God based on Higher Law. This was a big change and a great help to you, if you will see it with me.

Due to this decree about his people, Moses' Israelite mother had to make a little ark and hide him as a baby on the river near the palace, so that the Pharaoh's daughter might find him and favor him. You are familiar with the story. While the Pharaoh's daughter let another raise the child to a certain point, he still became her son.

Now this was Moses. This was his beginning. But his life was divided into three parts—of forty years each. The first part begins as I have described. Born to parents who were slaves, secreted in the bullrushes to escape death, he was rescued by the Pharaoh's daughter. This first period of his life signifies to us the need to overcome whatever limitations we found ourselves in at birth. Will you take time right now to forgive yourself once and for all for the limitations of your childhood, if there is this need? Or will you go on being just one of those who say, "Considering how my background was, the way I was born, and those who were around me, I have done pretty well, don't you think?"

To continue this first part of his life, Moses' tutorship at the royal court of Egypt as the adopted son of Pharaoh's daughter—also tells us something. It tells you and me that we should give to our intellect a trained mind while we are growing up. Moses had the best intellectual education possible in that day.

Then, as a young adult, remembering his real people, he killed in anger an Egyptian tormentor of his race. Therefore he was forced to flee the country. This signifies something quite different. The later accomplishments of Moses, showing what he became despite this tragedy, reveal this to us. So take it home to yourself. It means our mistakes during adolescence can be wiped out and prevented from destroying us. Moses proved this, and it is a lesson for all of us. It also signifies that attempting to garner justice by force, as Moses did, is immature. Have you been that route?

So you see the first part of Moses' life has much to offer us. It tells us: Clean up your birth, your background, your limitations. Get as much training for your intellect as possible. Whatever mistakes you have made, they can be wiped out. This is what Moses has contributed here.

Now we go to the second period of Moses' life —where so many people fail. In this second period, he had to flee his familiar part of the country. He became first a shepherd—then a leader of men. This period in his life also relates itself richly to us. Before Moses could attain true stature in leadership, the lonely hours as a shepherd provided ample time for silence, for meditation, for prayer. Beyond intellectual tutoring, beyond the trained intellect, have time for your God through prayer, meditation and silence to garner spiritual knowledge. This is a MUST for man. Such is what this part of Moses' life is saying to us. We see through this second period that a trained mind must also learn to see the invisible. To live from the great invisible Being—God. To be His manifesting nature. To see what God wants done. And do it!

You will remember, that in particular Moses depended on God for his words, for his direction, for the things that he had his people do. Not only the Ten Commandments came out of this, but judgments as to social conduct and ordinances for civil life—a tremendous array of great results. Yes, he learned to think from the Invisible Being of God, whom he represented as His manifesting nature. He learned to let God's Word be his word

—God's act, his act. He knew the Real Self, others just talked about—the Self of God individualized within him, the I AM.

This second period, then, makes very clear that we must set aside time for meditation and realization of spiritual things. That this is a MUST for living. The nine plagues are also in this second period. They are very interesting. They help you to read the Bible correctly. If you read the Bible the way it is written, it sounds as though God caused the plagues to make the Pharaoh and the Egyptians release the Israelites. Of course, that was simply the level of unfoldment of the people at that time in the Bible. That was their superstition. That was their ignorance at this particular moment.

What the Bible is really saying is that the Pharaoh and his people went against God by what they were doing, and brought the trouble upon themselves. When they said they would give up going against God, and did not, they got into further trouble and another plague came. What was true of Pharaoh and the Egyptian people is true of you and me. When we go against God, trouble comes. When we just ignore that we have gone against God, think it will just go away—it gets worse. We get into more trouble. Life is peculiarly arranged. We all have to change, and make an adjustment back to God. But some of us are tougher than others. And life is so arranged as to keep beating us and beating us—like Job— until we say, "There must be an easier way to live." And there is. Get back to God. That is what misuse of life is saying, and that is a great help— if you are open!

Now the last plague was a tremendous one. The last plague was the tenth. It was the one in which the first born of the Israelites and the first born of their cattle were to be slain. Moses was led to tell his own people, the Israelites, to do this: Take a lamb and sprinkle its blood on your door. Then this last plague will pass over you. The killing of your children will not happen. The killing of your cattle will not happen. Out of this grew the great ceremony known as the "Passover."

So this miracle took place. There were no deaths to the Israelites or their cattle—only to the Egyptians. This was the last plague. Again, it produced what is known as the "Passover." Many people, who are not of Hebraic background, think the "Passover" refers to the Red Sea Miracle. When Moses opened a path through the Red Sea, the Israelites went across and the Egyptians, that followed, sank. However, that miracle came after the tenth plague. The "Passover" refers to that moment when the Israelite children, first-born, and the first of the cattle, were not struck down by the tenth and last plague—only the Egyptians. This was the miracle of the "Passover," and that is its factual meaning.

But the relation of the "Passover" to you— means this. When you are in Truth, there should be such a regeneration and purification of your consciousness, it should spread through the doorway of your consciousness and blazon forth freedom for you from every plague of the world. This is what you should get out of the "Passover." Everything that happens in the Bible—to any personality or any event—relates to you. Truth is regenerating you. Truth is purifying you. It is the "Passover" sign on the doorway of your consciousness. Dr. Irvin Seale, used to say, "The essence of Truth is that you should keep the top of the kettle of your consciousness on to the world and open to God." Then, if your kettle of consciousness is challenged, only good will come out of it. That is what the "Passover" really means for you and for me!

Now for the final period, and this is that with which we shall end. The final period is the period of the Israelites wandering in the wilderness forty years—with Moses leading them. They got over the Red Sea, and they are on their way. You would think everything now would be rosy for them. No! There are times they did not have water to drink. Times they did not have food. These people, who previously adored Moses, began to say, "At least in slavery we got water. At least in slavery we had three meals a day. (Or whatever they were afforded in Egypt). Out here in this wilderness there is nothing, and you are to blame." Of course, no one does that today. That was way back when people did not know any better.

Moses had to do something about it. The way the story goes, he carried this special rod about with him. When he held it up and smote the rock, the water came forth for their thirst—at least they were shown how to sweeten bitter tasting water. When he held it up again, another miracle—the food, the "manna" came.

The essence of this story is interesting. Forty years in the wilderness, we are told. Yet it was not much longer a trip than from New York City to Buffalo. It would take no more than a few weeks at most for anybody walking. Why forty years? The Israelites needed to be processed from slavery to free people once again. They had been living on the dregs of life. Do you understand? These great people had gone down into slavery, and had to come back. Moses had to process them. As a great soul, he knew this intuitively from God!

Moses led them and held up a rod as a form of prayer for their water and for their food. The Bible tells us that at times he grew weary of raising up the rod, praying for the whole lot. He had to have help, so his brother, Aaron, and another began to help him hold it up. All of which meant that they helped him hold up the prayer work when he grew weary.

Finally he got to Mount Sinai, later referred to as Mount Horeb, and brought down the Ten Commandments to his people. The main thing is that he brought home to all of us the Higher Law of God!

Let me state how great that is, once you understand. This is the change that has happened in you. Your faith has been vitalized and made strong in God, because of this new understanding brought through by Moses. This means God operates by Law—not whimsy—not prejudice. When your consciousness has a vitalized faith such as this—if you really give yourself to God, open yourself positively to Him, see what He is doing and expect that to happen—God has no recourse but to do that. Yes, heal the eyes, heal the cells, stir up prosperity, procure the work, establish order in the family, bring forth justice, raise a slow period in your life to new activity. God has to do it! Knowing God operates by Law, not whims—faith and work are vitalized, because it is prayer prayed aright and not awry any longer.

I close with this: The Promised Land that Moses talked about for his people—is for all times and for all people. It is always already prepared for you, peculiar to your needs. It has been established by our Almighty God since the foundations of the world. You are not a cork cast out upon the ocean to be tossed hither and yon. He, who created you, did so to sustain you

—with an eternal Promised Land of abundant health, happiness, prosperity and success!

Spiritual Meditation

The lives of Abraham, Isaac, Jacob and Joseph are typical of some of the experiences through which we pass ere we stand on the firm ground that comes from the understanding of Higher Law. This Law was not revealed to Abraham. His sustaining power—was faith. But eventually faith must have as its foundation the understanding of God as "Lord" or Law. This was brought home to us by MOSES!

Moses' life was divided into three periods: That of being hidden away during childhood, yet educated at the royal court of Egypt when grown. That of serving as a shepherd of sheep as well as leader of his people. And finally that of wandering in the wilderness.

Let the FIRST period inspire you to overcome the limitations of your birth. Wipe out the mistakes of adolescence. And respect your intellect to the point of developing a trained mind. But let the SECOND period make you realize that intellectual knowledge alone will not suffice. That to it spiritual knowledge must be added through quiet study and realization of spiritual things. Finally, let the THIRD period make clear to you that leaving the negative beliefs in lower law for Higher Law is not done in one fell swoop. When bewildered, then let gentle persistence in knowing what God wants done and open-mindedness to His results—keep you steadfastly on The Path.

"And he believed in Jehovah (or Lord or Law); and he reckoned it to Him for righteousness."

Amer. Std., Genesis 15:6

OLD TESTAMENT

PART VII.

"THE TEN COMMANDMENTS
OR
THE DECALOGUE"

1. "Thou shalt have no other gods before Me."
2. "Thou shalt not make unto thee any graven image."
3. "Thou shalt not take the name of Jehovah thy God in vain."
4. "Remember the sabbath day, to keep it holy."
5. "Honor thy father and thy mother."
6. "Thou shalt not kill."
7. "Thou shalt not commit adultery."
8. "Thou shalt not steal."
9. "Thou shalt not bear false witness against thy neighbor."
10. "Thou shalt not covet."

Exodus 20:3 thru 17

Here we are going to do some tremendous work on ourselves. To do so, we are going to consider, "The Ten Commandments" or "The Decalogue," which so many know quite well. But, we are going to consider IN DEPTH these ten steps into Higher Law, that which perhaps you have never figured out—the metaphysical interpretation. The spreading, the expansion, the inclusion of these ten great Laws into your life—in depth—should prove highly interesting to you!

The Commandments, of course, are found in Exodus, Chapter 20, Verses 3 through 17. Here we have the literal meaning of them done on the severe basis of "Thou shalt not" for people on a primitive level—then and NOW. But, being the first revelation of the Lord of God or the Higher Law of God, they also contain a deeper, inner spiritual meaning for those who are ready to receive it.

Therefore, while we will consider briefly their literal meanings. Basically, we shall dwell upon their instructions, metaphysically interpreted, for our present day unfoldment. And it is a great joy to share this with you.

The First Commandment reads, "Thou shalt have no other gods before Me." It was worded that way, then, because the people had formerly in their tradition worshipped many gods. When the new One God seemed to fail them, it is understandable that it was easy for them to revert to old gods many. Moses, you will remember, found his people doing just that when he came down from the mountain, bringing the Ten Commandments.

Strangely enough, the literal meaning of the opening Commandment could well apply today, particularly to those, who in their intellectual sophistication, think of themselves as something apart from any kind of Deity. Who worship their beginning only as a Cosmic Accident. Who worship only dialectical materialism. Who consider only the findings of science. Who make these their gods!

However, for the Truth student of today— the deep, inner, spiritual meaning of the opening Commandment reaffirms his foundation premise for living. Even as the First Commandment reads, "Thou shalt have no other gods before Me." Even so, the basic premise for every Truth student is, "There is but one Presence and one Power in the universe, God, the good, omnipotent."

Often we will need to affirm this foundation premise of our lives, "There is but one Presence and one Power in the universe, God, the Good, omnipotent." This premise rests not on blind faith, but understanding faith. Spiritual, intuitional reasoning has made us to know certain things that relieve us and free us.

For example, spiritual, intuitional reasoning has made us to know that the devil is only the lower self, believing in lower law. Yes, that the devil is just the old in-a-rut you—caught up in lower laws and beliefs. Our understanding, as Truth students, has made us to see clearly that the product of this old in-a-rut self of us is the only evil or limitation we experience in our lives.

Where we are caught in a rut, we have the belief of limitation in self. So, in each instance of such limitation or frustration, you and I, as

Truth students, must learn to repeal in our consciousness the particular lower law of belief that has produced our trouble. When we have a trouble out here, we have a trouble within us. We are clouded. We need to put ourselves once again under the spell of the Higher Law. To do that, we must give this side of our life to Higher Law. Place it under Higher Law. What we belong to there in God. And gently insist on it in prayer. This is the way, we, as Truth students, break from the clutches of lower law.

I will put it another way. The essence of being a Truth student is to repeal every limited law under which you find yourself—at birth or at any other time in life. Repeal it by giving yourself to Higher Law. What you belong to in God. Gently insisting upon it until your consciousness changes to that. Until the troubled thing out here dissipates, and in its place God's way of life appears.

There is a marvelous passage in the Bible which enables and helps us to do this. Maybe you are acquainted with it, maybe you are not. In effect, it goes like this, "I the Lord am holy, and have severed you from other people, that ye should be Mine." (Leviticus 20:21). Now here is the inner meaning of that passage. "People" here symbolizes the negative conditions in our lives. Yes, I will sever you from the limited conditions produced by people. So stop saying, "Such conditions are the common lot of man— therefore, they are mine, too." Remember, "I will sever you from (such) people. . . ." Evil is simply the opinions of men demonstrated.

Now our spiritual sword that does this severing—is again our basic premise as Truth students, "There is but one Presence and one Power in the universe—God, the good, omnipotent." Yes, then, "Surely (only) goodness and mercy shall follow us all the days of our lives." Through this foundation premise, used often— that goodness and mercy shall seek us out and successfully find us. Thus, I have helped you to a modern-day usage of the First Commandment. "Thou shalt have no other gods before Me."

The Second Commandment reads, "Thou shalt not make unto thee a graven image." It was worded that way, then, long years ago; because the people, in reverting to old gods,

sought to give these gods form, THAT THEY
COULD SEE, by making "images" out of them
—"images" out of stone and metal.

Let us see where we are today. The rabbit's
foot, other lucky charms advertised in maga-
zines, magic stones picked up in India or wherever—these are the "carry overs" of this old-
time practice. Getting something that you can
make a graven image of represents this kind of
god for you. Yes, something you can get hold of,
look at and believe in—because it is physical.

Since the Truth student of today has none of
this in him, he does not need the rabbit's foot,
the lucky charm, the magic stone. He does not
need these "gimmicks" because he looks to a
deeper, inner, spiritual meaning of the Second
Commandment. And this is that on which we
are going to dwell.

What does he find—the real Truth student?
It instructs him to make no "graven image" out
of an accident to his body or a deep sickness that
has come upon him in the past. It instructs him
to make no "graven image" out of a loss of fortune in business. It instructs him to make no

"graven image" out of a mistake in the past—
until it has become a precedent for the rest of his
life. The real Truth student knows that he must
forgive himself. That God, in turn, then may
make that experience as though it had not happened! (Read my booklet, "Alter Your Past.")

The Second Commandment also cautions the
real Truth student against making a "graven
image" of possessions in his life. He knows that
it is possible to accrue so many, that pretty soon
one lives for his possessions. This is not to
demean them. We all need a certain amount of
possessions. Just do not let them possess you.
After all, the law of life is change! And we must
always make room—for it to be better.

Here is the Third Commandment, "Thou
shalt not take the Name of Jehovah thy God in
vain." It was worded that way, then, because
the people—when they felt God had let them
down—used His Name in a profane sense for
the purpose of expressing contempt.

Today, amusingly enough, when a person
uses the word "God" or "Deity" in a profane
sense, he does not do it intentionally as an

expression of contempt. Rather, as a swear word he has picked up to express frustration.

"Christ" is the New Testament term for God individualized in man, just as "Jehovah God" in Genesis is the term for God individualized in man. It might be added here for understanding's sake and for future reference in this lesson —that the "I Am" revealed to Moses also referred to God individualized in man. In other words, these three terms, "Jehovah God," "Christ" and "I Am" mean the same thing— God individualized in man!

A Truth student today is not fooled into believing that if he carefully avoids the use of "God," "Jehovah God," "Christ" or "I AM" as a swear word or phrase expressing frustration— he has completely complied with the Third Commandment. A Truth student knows better. He looks to the deeper, inner, spiritual meaning of this Commandment, and lets it instruct him against a worse usage of profaning God or His individualization. Such as, "I am sick. Well, maybe I am not sick, but I am never really well, either. I never know from day to day." That is truly profaning God because it is blaspheming the Holy One within self. "I am poor or a 'have not' is another profaning practice. Why? Because again it is limiting the Holy One within self. That is continuing in the rut you are in—the devil's road.

Here is another one, "Never got the breaks—" which is a sure way of keeping the "breaks" from your door in the future. For that is closing the door, closing the curtain. Here is another one, "I am a hot-water baby." A lady told me that years ago. I did not accept it. But she claimed it for herself. Then to make sure I understood, she said, "That means I have been in trouble all my life, ever since I can remember. Not only am I always in trouble, but I get everybody with whom I become involved—in trouble also. Yes, I am a real hot-water baby." Now that is indeed an unlovely thing to walk around with about self.

Since the Truth student of today readily understands the Name of God to mean the Nature of God—he also readily appreciates the fact that such misusages as I have enumerated represent the most important profaning of God. Which, of course, no person can afford to do. Yes, whatever you do to put the "damper" on God's Name or Nature—that eternally seeks its own level of excellence in you—is simply to be a fool. Such is the real meaning of "Thou shalt not take the Name (or the Nature) of Jehovah thy God in vain."

Here is the Fourth Commandment, "Remember the Sabbath Day to keep it holy." It was worded that way, then, isolated to a particular day, so that a primitive people would at least observe one day of the week. So it was good as far as it went.

That the primitive is still with us is testified to in so many ways. Here is one: A woman wrote me a letter to the effect that she was simply a week-end religionist. That the rest of the time she had to make a living. As though you could divorce Truth from your livelihood.

This woman typifies the religionist, who has not the slightest notion of the full possibilities of spirituality. That the individual can let his life be under Higher Law—ruled and enforced by the very Spirit of God. Supposedly on the surface, this is intended to be the goal of all religionists. But curiously—not in this lady's own language, "I am only a week-end religionist, you see, the rest of the time I have to make a living." In other words, it was not a full-time part of her life. Whereas, God, His Spirit, should be the prevailing influence in our lives, every day of our lives!

Thus the real Truth student of today—while he appreciates the reason why the Jewish religion sets aside Saturday as the Sabbath and the Christian religion sets aside Sunday—opens himself to the deeper, inner, spiritual meaning of the Fourth Commandment. It tells him that NO DAY must go without prayer. That prayer is a cycle of mental response Godward, which permits God to act in and through him to fulfill his needs. But that no such cycle is complete without its Sabbath. That this is the period of resting upon God's action, which one has initiated through his response in prayer. That this follow through of prayer is imperative.

The disciples once asked Jesus what are the signs that literally show you are praying effectively. He said in effect, "There are two. First, while you are in prayer you should feel a movement taking over, bigger than you have been, and in the direction of the fulfillment of your needs. Second, you should leave that prayer with a sense of resting upon that movement." Now this resting—is the Sabbath after each prayer. The real Truth student of today knows this resting upon the action of God, which prayer invoked, is as important as the prayer itself.

Next, the Fifth Commandment reads, "Honor thy father and thy mother." It was worded that way, then, because primitive man, which the people of that day were—being mired in slavery for so many years—showed little respect for parents.

Right adjustment in the realm of human relations begins with proper respect for the first persons we knew—our parents. Every form of psychology and psychiatry will constantly belabor this point: Find out how their lives were under their parents, and you will have a pretty good look at why they are the mess they are today.

That the primitive man or woman—then and now—needs this instruction is testified to by the fact that the primitive today in the depths of darkest Africa do away with their parents, when they reach a certain age and are no longer useful. Yes, the more primitive you are, the less inclined you are—to have a valid and real feeling about your parents when they are quite old.

But the Truth student of today, by the very nature of his unfoldment, automatically respects his earthly parents to the point of helping them—even if they may not be fully worthy of it. Why? Because he looks to the deeper, inner, spiritual meaning of the Fifth Commandment, which lies in his reverence for his heavenly parents, his Father-Mother God. The father quality in God teaches him wisdom. The mother quality in God teaches him love. This being his divine birthright—whether his earthly parents were able to do either!

The Sixth Commandment reads, "Thou shalt not kill." It was worded that way, then, because the more primitive man is, the cheaper is the price of life. That is the way it is with most primitive people in the world today—the muggers and the rapists. The wars of recent years also show that—the more primitive the people —the less value there seems to be on the individuals who have to go to war and die. Their leaders think nothing of sacrificing hordes of them to attain an insignificant military objective.

But the Truth student of today is the least primitive of all people in the world. And so he looks here to the deeper, inner, spiritual meaning of the Sixth Commandment—"Thou shalt not kill." It tells him, beyond physical murder, to be very careful not to destroy the courage and faith of another—for every man has the right to "life, liberty and the pursuit of happiness." This means that never must he, through personal will power amounting to a dominating personality, deprive another of this pursuit of life, liberty and happiness through utter domination. The Truth student knows he can figuratively kill another person by such dominion.

We, in the study of Truth, understand the true meaning of spiritual dominion. It does not mean to dominate anything or anybody. Rather it means to release or call forth in ourselves or another that which is divinely natural to us. That which belongs to us in God—that and nothing less. Such is the only dominion we were created to express.

This kind of understanding helps us in many ways as parents or in every day associations or whatever. It might sound strange to you but some mothers have actually told their daughters, "You could never do that," when the daughter wanted to try out for something. "Who do you think you are anyway?" they say. However, there are also mothers, who have such an inspired feeling about their children, that being president of the United States is not outside the realm of possibility.

There is something to be learned here. Let nothing in us kill another person's hopes. Let all that is within us encourage the other person. Let all that is within us encourage the other person to life in all its possibilities. This is the deep, inner, spiritual meaning of "Thou shalt not kill" to the Truth student of today.

The Seventh Commandment reads, "Thou shalt not commit adultery." And that is exactly what it meant, then. On the other hand, the more sophisticated the community today, the less likely would that be cause for disturbance. All of which reveals little to recommend the sophisticated in our society.

The real Truth student of today would have the least challenge from this particular Commandment in its literal sense. Because so much of his attention would always be on seeking a higher level of satisfaction for his life. Thus in reading this Commandment, he would seek beyond the literal meaning of the Commandment to its deeper, inner, spiritual meaning.

It would instruct him to see through challenges in his life to the potential expression of God. To him, then, the practice of seeing less— would be one of adulterating the "single eye of faith." His corrective approach to life would be, "See what the Father is doing" (what He wants brought into form here), and "Go and do likewise."

After all, the "Parable of Adam and Eve" makes it abundantly clear that we must not eat of the "tree of the knowledge of good and evil." It is just this "mixed fruit"—this adulteration— this mixture of good and evil in our thinking that brings our downfall. Not the total indulgence in negative thinking—which is too obvious! Rather it is the subtleness of our thinking in terms of both health and sickness, harmony and inharmony, prosperity and poverty—that fouls up our lives.

The Eighth Commandment reads, "Thou shalt not steal." It was worded that way, then, because man should not take that which is not his. And the more primitive the society, the more prevalent the practice. The real Truth student of today, being the least primitive by reason of his spiritual unfoldment, would have little tendency to take anything that is not his by right of consciousness. Because he knows that the only thing he can hold and make an integral part of his life is what he owns in consciousness —nothing more.

Thus he seeks the deeper, inner, spiritual meaning of this Commandment. It cautions him against the more subtle ways to steal. That, while the mental man is closer to the spiritual man than the physical or primitive man, yet the mental man leans to trickery. Thus while stealing is usually done through physical force, it is quite possible to do it by a more subtle form of force—namely—connivery, chicanery, deception, deviousness and flattery for the purpose of disarming and taking over.

The Ninth Commandment reads, "Thou shalt not bear false witness against thy neighbor." It was worded that way, then, because the less unfolded we are, the greater the tendency to bear false witness. The literal meaning of that is telling untruths about a neighbor. Much of gossip is a violation of this Commandment.

The real Truth student of today, by the very nature of his unfoldment, shies away from both these practices through a growing distaste for them due to that unfoldment. Thus he seeks an even higher application of this Commandment, its deeper, inner, spiritual meaning. It tells him that while he has every right, in any situation, to appraise the action as to whether it is right or wrong, on key or off—personal criticism and condemnation of the person INSTEAD OF HIS ACTIONS is nothing more than bearing false witness.

Another way of putting this Commandment for the deep Truth student is this: When the Bible says, in effect, "Judge not according to appearances but judge righteous judgment," it is a way of saying, "Stop bearing false witness about this person" (or just the negative facts about him). Yes, look past the outer appearance to what he still is or can be in Truth. This is the essence of being a Truth student. It frees you in your feelings about him and blesses him!

Also, "See what the Father is doing" (what God wants done through that person) and "Go and do likewise" (or become that in consciousness through prayer for him). In other words, do not treat the person but your idea of him—until every time you think of him you can free him into the God idea of him.

The Tenth Commandment reads, "Thou shalt not covet." It is worded that way, then, because coveting that which belongs to another is probably one of the most pronounced practices of the primitive person.

The real Truth student of today knows that most wars are fought because one nation covets that which belongs to another nation. He also is aware that avarice, envy, jealousy and selfishness in people are closely allied with covetousness.

Thus he seeks the deeper, inner, spiritual

meaning of this Commandment—above all, the answer that will free him from all forms of this vice—coveting that which belongs to another. And that answer, like all great answers and things, is simple. It goes like this: Never covet that which another has demonstrated. Be it the wife, the husband, the possessions, the land, the home, the car or whatever. Rather, be grateful to that person for showing you what you would like to have in your life. What you want—is not that thing, but its equivalent, which is prepared and waiting for you still in God. Yes, waiting for you to develop the response in consciousness to receive it.

Let us close with this realization:

The Ten Commandments stand, and always will stand, as sound, basic steps to spiritual unfoldment. Understanding them and comply- ing with them, then, is a must! And it needs to be pointed out—that it is impossible to seek out and comply with their deepest meaning without obeying them literally, too!

Spiritual Meditation

The Decalogue represents the first revelation of the Higher Law (Lord) of God to man or The

Ten Commandments. It is presented through Moses on the severe basis of "Thou shalt not," because this was the way it was needed to be presented at that time due to the level of man's unfoldment.

Nevertheless, The Ten Commandments stand today, and always will, as the foundation stones upon which our spiritual structure is built. They should be obeyed both in the letter and in the Spirit. Conformance to the letter alone is not enough. On the other hand, it is not possible to obey them in their highest spiritual sense, without obeying them literally, too.

Exodus 20:3 thru 17 contains The Ten Commandments. Their literal meanings were done on the severe basis of "Thou shalt not" for people on a primitive level then and NOW. But, being the first revelations of Higher Law or the Law of God, they have deeper, inner, spiritual meanings for those who are ready to receive them.

Therefore, while we have considered briefly their literal meanings, we have also dwelt upon their instructions, metaphysically interpreted, for a higher level of unfoldment. So we are now

about to meditate upon the depth of meaning
The Ten Commandments have for us in keeping
with that higher level of unfoldment. In other
words, the depth of meaning they may now
have for you will tell you much about yourself—how much you have grown through your
study of Truth!

NEW TESTAMENT

NEW TESTAMENT

PART I.

"BIRTH BY PROXY"

"Jesus . . . said unto him (Nicodemus), Verily, verily, I say unto thee, Except a man be born again, he cannot see the kingdom of God."   John 3:3

"Nicodemus saith . . . , How can a man be born when he is old? Can he enter the second time into his mother's womb, and be born again?"   John 3:4

"Jesus answered . . . That which is born of the flesh is flesh; and that which is born of the Spirit is Spirit."   John 3:6

"Blessed is she (Mary) that believed for there shall be a performance. . . ."   Luke 1:45

Remember the purpose of this book is to enable you to read the Bible in a most practical

161

way. To understand it. To make it really worthwhile in your life.

In all the highlights of the Old Testament we
saw ourselves in each personality and event dis-
cussed. We saw things to do, and things not to
do. This is the way to read the Bible.

This second half of the Bible, the New Testament, is still the story of you—in everything
that takes place. If you do not see yourself and
relate yourself to the episodes, events and characters—then you have read in vain. For the
whole of the Bible is what? The gradual INVO-
LUTION of God's Spirit in man. And then its
follow through, the gradual EVOLUTION of
that Spirit into form or demonstration.

Let us be reminded by the study we have
already made of the Old Testament, that without the glorious unfoldment attained there, our
continued unfoldment through the New Testament could not happen. So we are now going to
accomplish a growing unfoldment in our person
by considering the inception of the man upon
whom the New Testament is based, Jesus
Christ.

I have chosen as my subject for this segment, "Birth By Proxy." "Proxy" means authority to act for another. This historical story, while it happened to another person, cites exactly in detail what is necessary in you for the great Second Birth we are all after.

Let us preface the story by reviewing the influence of this particular man—as we did Abraham, Jacob, Joseph, and Moses.

The secret of Jesus' enduring influence lies in the ability of His teachings to stand the test of time. Also, in the demonstration of that which He taught—through His own person. And finally, in the fact that what he claimed for Himself he claimed for every man. Those are the three factors that lie behind His influence. All of this has never ceased to appeal to the potential divinity in all of us.

Jesus made us to realize something about the prophecies that forecast his coming. And there were several, you know, in the Old Testament. For He clearly represents an extension of the unfoldment that was already made. What was it He made us to realize? That all of the Hebrew

prophecies about His coming were descriptive
—of our own potential. That they are prophecies of the coming—of our Real Self—personalized for us by the man, Jesus Christ!

The name "Jesus Christ" has a two-fold
meaning, and it should be made precisely clear
to us. "Jesus" was the name of the man of Galilee. "Christ" was the descriptive term used to
depict the individualization of God in man as
Principle. It was not fully associated with Jesus
until somewhere in His last three years. Somewhere in the midst of those three years He was
finally called the Christ. The term, "Christ," is
a translation from the Greek. The Greeks called
it "Christos," the Greek term for the Hebrew
word, Messiah. Whom the Hebrew prophets
had prophesied would come; be revealed; and
made manifest by some individual.

So "Jesus," as such an individual, represents
the individualization of God in man as Principle
—made manifest! That which is finally going to
happen in us through the unfoldment we are
making. The word, "Christ," then—is the seed
of God in man. It is there mighty in the midst of
us. It is the potential Self of us, the Real Self. All
that it possesses exists in us now. It is a matter of

making ourselves ready to receive it. Being responsive enough to let it happen in this outer self of us.

In Jesus, therefore, we have the privilege of witnessing the outpicturing of the potential that resides within us. So this potential, Spiritual Self, abides in each one of us. And it does not matter how much or how little we have used it to date—it is there!

The "apostles," who surrounded Jesus, symbolize twelve spiritual powers, which add up to the whole of the "Christ" depicted by Jesus. Twelve great powers of God—that is a lesson in itself. Let me give you some idea of their possibilities in you.

One of these powers is the power of renunciation. A simple illustration of its use could be found in the old-fashioned, green, window blind, which was used to shut out the outer world immediately. Thus, if you have something you would like to sever yourself from—some habit, some influence, whatever— through the analogy, just think of that old-fashioned, green, window blind. That in pulling it down you are using this great power of renunciation. That through it you are severing yourself utterly from that which you would see dissolved from your life. Try it! The Bible refers to it in many ways. One such instance is, ". . . I the Lord am holy, and have severed you from other people, that you should be Mine." (Leviticus 20:26). The term "people" here used means any and all negative conditions of mankind—by which you would be conditioned.

If the possibilities of this power intrigue you, do not in practicing the power of renunciation try to jerk it down like the old window blind. The more gently you pull it down, the less you are interfering, the less you are trying to make the severing happen yourself. Then you are letting the power of renunciation do it. Remember, it has its own power! And it will do its own work!

The "Pharisees" and the "Sadducees" are rather obvious in this story of the birth of the "Christ" through the person of Jesus. They stand for the qualities in the human consciousness that oppose or resist this Real Self. The "Pharisee" is the religious type, who is lost in his religion, but has not found spirituality. He is noted for his strict observance of rites and ceremonies, and his insistence on the validity of traditions. The "Sadducee" denies any power within the individual to resurrect himself, and thus along with it, the possibility of personal immortality.

Our real potential nature was demonstrated by Jesus. Real spirituality is the continued expansion of the expression of God's Spirit, which you witnessed in Abraham, Jacob, Joseph, and Moses. The New Testament is a continuation of this. To paraphrase Paul, "We have indeed born the image of the earthly, but we shall also bear the image of the heavenly." Yes, this Spiritual Self that is within us—this Real Self—is inevitably a part of our future. And the time to show forth more of that Self is now!

This higher state of consciousness is possible to all who follow the Truth that Jesus advanced from the preceding prophets. He was first to acknowledge the work of the great ones, who went before Him. His favorite quotations were from the Psalms, if you will remember, showing how conversant He was with the great Truths that had come through before Him.

Now Jesus was our Saviour in this sense. In the same sense that Moses helped to save us from just being the human self. Jacob, too, revealed the physical, mental and spiritual levels of our being. Abraham showed us that we must always have a new land—a new goal that we would possess. Joseph taught us how to use the power of imagination spiritually. And all of them demonstrated that "Greater is He that is within us, than he that is in the world." So it was, then, that Jesus was our Saviour, as were the others, in the sense of being wayshowers to the "Christ," to this Real Self—that resides within us!

The four Gospels—Matthew, Mark, Luke and John—are biographies of Jesus. Each depicted Jesus as the biographer saw Him. Mark's gospel, for example, emphasizes Jesus' works more than His teaching. Mark was interested in that. What Jesus was able to do. The gospel of Matthew endeavoured to prove Jesus to be the

Messiah of Hebrew prophecies. It featured se-
lective groupings of His teachings. Luke's gospel
makes the most of Jesus as the Great Physician.
Why did this biographer write mostly of the
healings? Because he, himself, was a physician.
The gospel of John dramatizes Jesus as the Word
of God. You will remember how it starts out.
"In the beginning was the Word, and the Word
was with God, and the Word was God." Thus
we notice, it compares Jesus to the Word of God
—the "Word made flesh." The Word that we
now seek to release, and let become flesh or
form in our lives in keeping with our needs.

It is helpful here to remind ourselves again
that the Bible is a book symbolizing the involution of the Spirit of God in man, and the evolution of that Spirit through man into form. Thus
every episode that we review in the Bible,
whether it is a parable, an allegory or history
holds key instructions for our lives. And that is
the way we want to read it.

So it is, then, that the "narrative of the birth
of Jesus," the same as the "birth of Moses,"
interpreted metaphysically, reveals exact keys of

instruction. Let us meditate for a moment upon the key instruction that Mary, Jesus' mother, symbolizes. "Mary" symbolizes your own soul, magnifying the Lord, the Higher Law of your being, daily. Thus she symbolizes the devotion by which your soul prepares itself for the Higher Life.

By now you must know that the essence of the study of Truth is to repeal every lower law which you have picked up. Yes, any definite belief you have about your person that is negative. To repeal that, and in its place, allow God to write his Higher Law. That is what we are doing constantly and steadfastly in the study of Truth. Repealing the old, definite, negative beliefs, and taking on the new, definite, positive beliefs of what we belong to in God.

"Mary" also symbolizes the changing for the better of the emotional or feeling nature of your soul. We are told, "She pondered these things in her heart." Yes, in the emotional or feeling nature, which you, like Mary, are purifying until it becomes highly intuitive and sensitive to inspiration from God.

We are purifying our feeling nature so that gradually we are giving it back to that for which it was first created. Yes, in the beginning, God created you in such a way as to work directly upon your subconscious or feeling nature first. Then up to the canvas of your conscious mind. So that you would express only that which He wanted through you. But He gave us free will, and through that, we got lost in the outer. However, through the study of Truth, we are now giving our feeling nature back to God. We are making it intuitive and sensitive to what He wants done. To the Higher Plan, the Lord or Higher Law of God, the "life more abundant," that belongs to us.

Above all, in purifying and conditioning our subconscious so that God can work upon it directly again, we are constantly opening ourselves to more and more inspiration that makes us to know that we are bringing forth the Son, the Child of the Most high, from within us. Every problem, spiritually worked out, means a little bit more of the Real Self has become manifest. Boiled down it amounts to this: We have a Child within us—this Child of God that we are bringing up into adulthood through challenges.

Every challenge worked out by releasing the Action of the Real Self—God with us—not only handles the problem but also leaves us on higher ground. This is a good picture of our growth. The full coming forth of this Real Self, letting it be completely in charge of our life, is tantamount to the "life more abundant."

As to the "virgin birth" of Jesus—listen carefully. It should be accepted by you only in the sense that it was His divine origin. That it was this divine origin that gave him power—not the peculiar circumstances surrounding his physical birth. This correct perspective of the virgin birth should make you to know that you, too, are immaculately conceived in your divine origin. That this is also the reason for your power potential, regardless of your physical birth.

Remember Moses did not do great works until he saw "the burning bush," and from it realized the "I AM," the most literal wording of "God in man" to be found in the Bible. He was told to take off his shoes because he stood on Holy Ground, you will remember. The "shoes," or his limited human understanding, separated him from God. When he got onto the "I AM," this was the Second Birth for Moses, you see.

Jacob experienced such when he finally advanced over the physical man and from the mental man to the spiritual man. At long last "wrestling with the Man in the tent," who was his Real Self—and becoming that! So you see these experiences of both Moses and Jacob were descriptions of the same experience, which reached a peak through Jesus Christ. He, being able to reach that peak, because of the great work done by those who had gone before Him.

It is imperative, above all, that you know you bear the same relationship to God as Jesus or Moses or Jacob or any of these great souls. Jesus may have demonstrated more proof of His Sonship than you. Yet potentially you are equally God's Child. And that is the position from which to operate. That is the premise to take seriously and privately for your life. Not to be talked about, but lived. "Position," someone once said for emphatic emphasis—"is nine tenths of the game." In all sports, when you are in position, you play the game easier. Out of position, you are at a disadvantage.

Life is a game, too, and you must find your position, which is one of Sonship. Then the things of God flow easily to you. But not to one, who is constantly saying, "I am only human." Why? The human is too full of his limitations and his scars from out of the past.

In the process of bringing the potential of your Second Birth or Spiritual Birth into realization and manifestation, there is involved yet another faculty of your mind that will help you to utilize your Real Self. "Joseph"—not the prophet of the Old Testament—but the one betrothed to Mary in the story of the birth of Jesus, brings this faculty to our usage. He represents understanding, and such is greatly needed in assisting the birth of Christ in you.

For example, we are now dwelling upon the idea of the indwelling Christ in us. But this revelation of our Real Self must be protected and sustained, and that is done through understanding.

"Mary," you will remember, "pondered these things in her heart"—this coming great birth of the Son of God. But "Joseph," who represented

understanding, devotedly cared for Mary. He
devotedly cared for her ONCE HE UNDER-
STOOD CORRECTLY WHAT WAS TAK-
ING PLACE IN HER. And there we find great
help for ourselves. It means our understanding
must be devoted to this revealing of the Christ
—within self. As the Bible puts it in another
reference, ". . . He that keepeth understanding
shall find good." (Prov. 19:8).

Now, as the account of Jesus' life continues, it
should be with the perception that we are witnessing the unfoldment of our own individual
consciousness Godward. "Mary," again, symbolizes the purifying of the emotional nature of
our soul until it has become heavily charged
with the divine idea—this Real Self, the Christ.
But it needs to be unified even more with substance before there can be manifestation.

The story tells that Joseph took Mary to Bethlehem. That he went there to pay taxes. So
"Bethlehem" metaphysically signifies the relating of Mary to substance. She was the one who
was pondering this Real Self. But this pondering
had to be related to substance in order to get the
manifestation she was after. For us it means

simply that we must do the same. It means that from our position of the Real Self or the Christ, we must now let the life substance ("know how" from God for our body), love substance ("know how" from God for our human relations) and prosperity substance ("know how" from God for our supply) enter into our subconscious by setting up definite spiritual treatments in our lives to that end!

Next, we come to that part of the narrative with which you are so familiar. There was no place or "no room for them in the inn," when they got to Bethlehem. This, too, has a relation to you. It describes the worldly habitat where they were denied lodging. But it also symbolizes the worldly interest that has no place for spiritual things or no room for the divine idea to come forth. Worldly interest offers little help in letting the Real Self get a chance to come through. It takes quietness. It takes simplicity. We must have this in our spiritual meditation periods. That is when the Real Self comes forth easily.

So it is quite fitting in the narrative that Jesus, whose "birth" symbolizes this Real Self coming forth in us, was born—in a manger or cave or grotto—away from the inn of worldly interests and so forth.

Then, too, we are acquainted with the shepherds in the narrative. And we need to understand what the "shepherds," who were the first to pay homage to the infant, represent in us. They symbolize the part of you that has faith in God. That is the part of you, working with the Real Self. That is the part of you, paying homage to the Real Self. So the shepherds were the first to pay homage. The shepherds in you are again what? That part of you having faith in God. Only you know how much of yourself really believes in God as yet.

When you are obedient to the revelation of the Christ or the Real Self in you, willing to let that Real Self take charge of your life and affairs; then that Real Self becomes the Saviour of your personal world.

"Herod" in the story, if you remember, was appointed by the Roman Emperor in 40 B.C. to be the ruler of the Jews. He was not well liked. He was also afraid of the people. Being informed that Bethlehem, according to the prophecy, was the place where this infant was to be born, he sent wise men with instructions to go to Bethlehem to see if this birth was taking place. Should they find the child, they were to come back to him to tell him. He would then supposedly go and pay homage to the infant child himself. But that was not his real intention. He planned to slay the infant. Why? Because he was so afraid the Child would be a threat to his rule.

What does "Herod" represent in us? It is easy to blame it all on Herod, you know. That terrible person way back there, who was going to slay this infant Child. Then turn the page to see what comes next. Thus we miss the whole point. No, you must take time to relate this episode to yourself. "Herod" symbolizes the ruling will of your physical self. Yes, the ego of your sense consciousness, which ever seeks to destroy the spiritual as a threat to its rule.

For example, suppose you have a physical condition. That negative condition first had to become a belief in your subconscious before it could manifest in your body. Now you are releasing the Grace or Action of the Real Self in you by its Word—for the cleansing of your subconscious from that belief. You definitely know that the Word of the Real Self, releasing this Action, is superior to the belief. Thus is dissolving it, and writing the Higher Law of wholeness there. Well, that old negative belief in you, which had its physical counterpart—is like "Herod." It would slay this Action of the Real Self in you released by the Word. It would stop it. But you will not let that happen. You will persist in speaking the Word for your body. This is today's business in you!

The same thing must be done in human relations. Again, the same thing must be done in matters of business, supply and success. Remember, though, the healing is always first in your subconscious for your body. The healing is always first in your subconscious for your human relations. The healing is always first in your subconscious for your business. Then the outer condition straightens out! Just remain spiritually willing. Do not let "Herod"—any negative belief from out of your physical self— stop this great ongoing Action of the Real Self, released through its Word—prevent the healing you need. Yes, "Let the weak say I am strong," the Bible tells us. By like token, let those suffering inharmony say, "My human relations are being established in divine order now." And finally, let those experiencing lack say, "I am being prospered in all ways until only sufficiency and to spare exist in my affairs."

Now the "wise men of the east" in the story have a two-fold meaning. The "east" in the Bible always means the direction from whence comes the spiritual. Thus it represents the deep spiritual within of you. The "wise men" represent the wisdom from the deep, spiritual within of you that rises to the surface, when its depths are stirred by a great revelation.

With Mary the revelation was the Son of God —this Real Self coming forth. With you the revelation is the same, plus the goals you are working out through that Self. With this revelation, all the wisdom of the spiritual deep of you comes to the fore to work with you on these goals.

Next in the story—"gifts" were poured out upon the Christ Child by the wise men, you will remember. These "gifts" reverse themselves and represent, in turn, what the Christ or the Real Self of you will pour out now upon you as you take a greater hold of that Self. Yes, as you pay homage to your Real Self with your gifts of attention, responsiveness, expectancy, praise and thanksgiving, that Self, in turn, pours out ever more of this Higher Action upon you to heal your body, harmonize your relations and prosper your affairs. That is—when you make that Real Self the center of your life, as these wise men did.

The "gifts" they (the wise men) poured out were what? "Gold," which symbolizes the riches of the Spirit. "Frankincense," which signifies the beauty of the Spirit. And "myrrh," which stands for the eternity of Spirit. The Spirit of God, you know, is the means by which God acts through man.

So for the "life more abundant," you must be born again. This Real Self, taking full possession of your life, is tantamount to the "life more abundant." Here, in this lesson, you have had a unique chance to witness the birth of this Real Self coming to the fore in you—DONE BY PROXY! The story, as given to you, represents keen points for releasing more of the Christ through you. Letting more of the Real Self take charge of your life. You have witnessed these points one at a time. Through each—you have taken on the feeling that you have grown. Believe it! Stay with it! So that whatever goals you may have in your life—will now be consummated easily—without stress, strain or will power. Why? Because yours is now spiritual willingness to let ONLY God's will, in and through you, be done!

Spiritual Meditation

"Ye must be born again," Jesus told us in effect. But how? Here is your chance to witness it DONE BY PROXY. That is, by somebody else for you. Always remember, once a thing is done, there is a way in which it was done. And that way can be yours! Every episode in the Bible, whether it be a parable, an allegory or history, symbolizes key instructions for your life.

So it is, then, that the "narrative of the birth of Jesus," metaphysically interpreted, reveals exact keys of instruction for the birth of Christ in you.

As a start, and for the purpose of conditioning ourselves to the full lesson we have read, let us meditate for a few moments upon the key of instruction that Mary, Jesus' mother, symbolizes.

"Mary" symbolizes your own soul, when it MAGNIFIES the Christ, your Real Self, daily in the temple of your own being through prayer—even as your soul is doing now!

The Christ can only be born through the mind of man. To be self impregnated with an idea is to conceive it. If the "I" in man is lifted up to a higher level of consciousness through the I AM or Christ or Sonship, his expressed world must change. The things of God flow easily to the Son, when man assumes the things of the Son. So stop saying, "After all, I am only human." Then the dam, the wall, the debris of the human is removed—and the things of the Son just flow into their proper places. Let that happen now!

NEW TESTAMENT

PART II.

"JOHN THE BAPTIST, JESUS AND YOU"

The Keystone of John The Baptist

"Repent ye; for the kingdom of heaven is at hand."   Matthew 3:2

"And now also the ax is laid unto the root of the trees: every tree therefore that bringeth not forth good fruit is hewn down, and cast into the fire."   Luke 3:9

The Keystone of Jesus The Christ

". . . I am come that they might have life, and that they might have it more abundantly."   John 10:10

"Be not overcome of evil, but overcome evil with good."   Romans 12:21

We are now going to enter into our subject, "John The Baptist, Jesus And You." A secondary title, which really expresses the heart of what I am after is—"The Maturing Christ in You."

This segment has much to offer us as we move along into the New Testament. Basically, it has to do with the maturing of the Deeper Self of you. It is not enough to know that the names— I AM, Jehovah God and Christ—all mean the same thing. It is not enough to put them all into one hamper and call them your Deeper Self. That does not make you superior. That just gives you a little edge. You simply now do not have to wade through so much—as others do.

It is like Marconi, who invented the wireless. They marveled at him because he was able to bring wireless through at such a young age. He answered in effect, "Well, all my competitors thought there would be resistance to meet, but I simply knew there was no resistance in the air to overcome. Thus I had quite an early advantage over the others."

With comparable simplicity, should you put all terms for the Deeper Self into one package, you make it easier for yourself. But more than that, we are now interested in this period in the Bible for maturing the usage of that Deeper

Self, so that we can get much greater returns, much greater results.

The first stage of your spiritual maturity into the Christ or Deeper Self is symbolized by Jesus' first announcement of His dedication to God's service. After all, everything Jesus achieved, He accomplished by the Christ or this Deeper Self —and it is just as much in you as in Him. At twelve years of age He uttered this pronouncement, "Wist ye not that I must be about my Father's business?" What He was saying here was—He intended to put God first for the rest of His life.

Now I do not know at what moment and what age you have made such a dedication. But it is required of one in this study—that you do so. Not something just to declare to others, but as a private and sacred thing. That you may understand once and for all that you represent a Being greater than yourself.

The great moment that is now coming in the involution of God's Spirit and its evolution into form through you—is the emphasis upon this great Truth. That it is the Father within that doeth the work in the working out your goals spiritually. Not just you going through some mental manipulations.

It is true that you do in the outer everything that comes to you to consummate these working outs. But you have the sense of being very intuitive now. That what is coming to you in the way of guidance is coming from the Father. That you are acting out what He wants done. That His great power moves in and through you to bring about the healing or position or harmony or order or protection you may need.

Now get that picture. So, if you have not had the real sense before of dedicating your life to God, let it begin: "I represent a being greater than I. It is the Father within me, the Deeper Self, that doeth the work. For the rest of my life, I shall put Him first. Through the working out of each of my goals, a little more of Him comes forth through me." Here we have a sense of really working with God for the rest of our lives. Putting Him first. What He wants done.

Here is the point I want to emphasize: That this
is a stage in the Bible of maturing—the Deeper
Self in you!

Thus we come to John The Baptist. He had a
very special place in the Bible—for Hebrew and
Christian people alike. More and more I wish
that religion would do away with the practice
of separation. Get to the fact we are all just
God's children. Going in one direction—to
manifest Him. That is all.

Now John The Baptist formed the connecting
link between Judaism and Christianity by his
recognition of Jesus as the Messiah—long promised by some Hebrew prophets. Perhaps the
greatest one was Isaiah, who in my mind had
the deepest intellectual hold on Truth of any
writer in the Old Testament. He has much to
say about this "coming." This coming, though,
must not be confined just to the man, Jesus. The
vision was that sooner or later someone would
come, who would personify that which is individualized IN US ALL—the Christ.

This happened to a degree through Moses. He
was not able to do anything of magnitude until

he came to realize that this Deeper Self was the real part of him. He knew it by the name "I Am."

Jacob, too, was getting nowhere in life. Superior to the physical, he could match wits with the mental. But he never found the full answer to life until he wrestled all night in his tent with a "Man" for his final overcoming. That "Man" was this Deeper Self.

Abraham became great because he recognized a covenant given to him by One greater than himself. The One he was representing. And he finally followed it through. The same with Joseph.

Everything we have read in the Old Testament brought us keys to our own advancement. And this leads us to something very clear. That the way to our highest good is best found through "That Something" within us—that is there of God. This Deeper Self spells the difference. Otherwise, we are just going a mortal way of trying to find the full meaning of life.

Now we have John The Baptist putting a

bridge together to make us know for sure that what we have been studying in the Bible is the gradual, greater unfoldment or outpicturing of this Deeper Self through us. John bore witness to this Deeper Self in Jesus. Made manifest in a more pronounced fashion than had ever happened. For which Abraham, Jacob, Joseph and Moses were forerunners.

"John The Baptist," witnessing this Deeper Self possessing a person more fully than had ever been seen—represents illumined intellect. So here, you too must see your intellect illumined to bear witness to this.

An illumined intellect means one that is turned toward spiritual things. John had to be anticipating. Had to be aware that Jesus was someone that must happen. That He was coming to show the way, more so than ever before!

You already are aware of this Deeper Self. You are an illumined intellect, because you anticipate far more results from this Deeper Self in you than you ever have before. This is a period in which you are galvanizing all of your anticipation to this Deeper Self.

Now "Zachariah" comes to the fore, as we move along here. He was a priest of Judea, and he was the father of John The Baptist. His particular portion in this spiritual unfoldment of ours is something a little different than John's. He had a great deal, but he represents a tendency to be dumbfounded as to how God is going to solve a problem. Yet he rejoiced when God did. You may recognize this in yourself.

John The Baptist's mother is also interesting. Her name was Elizabeth. Mary, as you know, was the mother of Jesus. These two mothers were cousins showing that John The Baptist and Jesus, who finally and fully revealed this Deeper Self, were related.

That tells us something metaphysically. As we watch John giving way to Jesus, it tells us that the intellect in its highest state is closely connected to the spiritual. We witnessed that in Jacob, you will remember from the Old Testament—who gradually became Israel. Yes, the illumined intellect is the nearest state to the spiritual.

As we go over this you should be asking yourself, "Just about where am I in this picture?"

Now the keynote of John The Baptist's message was special. He represents something in you—going in the right direction. His keynote basically was, "Repent ye for the Kingdom of heaven is at hand."

We need to understand how important that was. Orthodox religion of John's day, more or less believed the kingdom was going to be out here on earth; and John's followers, by being of that particular group, automatically would belong to that belief. John, who was one of them, said in effect, "Oh, no, you have to repent. You cannot be a mess, and still get into heaven. You have to get rid of the conditions of your consciousness that are fouling up your life." As Truth students, we have already faced that harsh Truth.

I was recently speaking to someone about a mutual friend for whom I was treating. I said, "There is still some left of the old law about that part of her body—a belief that she has. No amount of materia medica is going to change that cause. It has to be cleaned out. But it is going. It is less. It appears fainter. So it is being cleaned up. And in its place the Word of God, the Higher Law, is being written in her inward parts, bringing perfect function eventually to that part of her body."

This is the meaning of repentance. It means the illumined intellect understands that a change must take place within our own consciousness. We must give something up. It amounts to this: Some people would love to be in heaven as far as their problem is concerned, but they have not as yet made up their mind to give up their hell. So we have to make a decision. Which way are we going?

This change must take place before the kingdom can become a reality. Change here means turning from the materialism of your condition and reaching for the spiritual idea that belongs there. That which God wants done.

Now when you talk about The Baptist, and that was part of John's name, or the name appended; you must consider what baptism means, and why it is part of his name. Let us understand once and for all what spiritual baptism really is. Do you know what it is? You say, "Oh, yes, that is one of the rites of a church.

Some sprinkle and some don't. Some have other mysterious methods, and I do not know whether I want to go through that or not." No, that is just a form. In many, many instances it does not "take," as you well know.

Spiritual baptism, in its real meaning, is much more than that. It means the baptizing of your subconscious with the "Truth that sets free." And everyone who is studying Truth is gradually baptizing his subconscious with the Truth—idea by idea.

You do understand that the only thing you ever demonstrate is the contents of your subconscious mind, do you not? That your conscious mind does not demonstrate a "thin dime." Only as you gather knowledge, good or bad, and let it become a conviction in your subconscious— only then do you own it. When that happens, you demonstrate it!

So we may say real spiritual baptism, then, is the baptizing of your subconscious with the "Truth that sets free." All right! This is attained —and you need to understand it—first through repealing the false beliefs from the world that have become convictions in your subconscious. Never mind where you got them. Whether from relatives, friends, observations, tragedies you have been through, and so forth. Some people date themselves to the time they had an accident. The time they had something of a mental breakdown or whatever. It is a deep scar with them. Their life begins for them there. Whatever took place, repeats itself, because they constantly keep it up to date in their memory.

Now these negative beliefs we need to repeal —have become laws of our consciousness. Yes, when you really believe something negative, it becomes a law to your personal life. But the glorious thing about that is—it harms you only as long as you believe it. The moment someone helps you to see you do not have to go on that way—if you are willing to give it up—you are free. It is very much like a person being in prison for nine years, who had cried his eyes out over his predicament. But finally one day he happened to lean on the door, and found to his amazement that it was not locked. Nine years he had been there suffering. That is all such belief is—a prison. It keeps you there only as long as you believe it.

Part of baptism is what, then? The repealing of whatever false beliefs you have about your body, that have become laws for your body. Whatever false beliefs you have about your business, that have become laws for you there. Whatever false beliefs you have about human relations, that have become laws for that side of your life.

Some people are very much like the flea, you know, that is trained for the circus. The trainer puts it in a little glass box. And it jumps. That is its nature, you know. But the trainer arranges a low ceiling so that it hits its head. When the flea realizes it cannot jump that high without hurting its head, it begins to jump just so high and no more. Then the trainer releases it from the box confident it will perform that way in the circus—without benefit of the box.

And so it is with you. These beliefs you have just trained yourself to be—represent the essence of where you are to date. So baptism is the repealing of those lower laws that you picked up from somewhere, plus the instillment in their stead—of God's Higher Laws for your life.

Basically, it requires your willingness to let go —and let God write His Higher Laws in you. You see, the word "Lord" when used for God, means also all the Higher Laws of God. If you were going to Harvard and studying law, you would not say, "I am going to Harvard— and studying laws." You would say, "I am studying law." So it is in the Bible, you are studying the "Lord." In so doing, you are studying the Higher Law for all sides of your life— God's plan for your life. Jesus was finally called the Lord simply because He demonstrated it, and thus personalized it for us all.

The baptism that is taking place in you through the study of Truth is simply this: Little by little these Higher Laws—what you belong to in God—are "taking" in your subconscious. And the old laws, that you picked up from the world, through friends, relatives, observations, accidents and so forth, are being repealed.

If anyone asks you whether you have been baptized, do not get into an argument about it. Just know that you have been and are continuing to be—in the most real way.

Various forms of baptism simply symbolize the real thing. John The Baptist represented water baptism, which symbolizes the cleansing of all old limited beliefs. Thus that is its meaning. Jesus represented the needed follow through, the instilling of the Truth ideas of the Higher Laws. Jesus baptized by Holy Spirit, you will remember; John baptized by water. They are both good. One is a cleansing of the lower laws, and the other is the letting in of the Higher Laws.

John spoke of this, you know, because Jesus came to him to be baptized. John quickly discerned in Jesus that He had already become this Deeper Self. So John substantiated his own water baptism in this way. He said, "I indeed baptize you in water unto repentance . . . But He (Jesus) will baptize you in Holy Spirit." John said of Jesus, "I have need to be baptized of Thee," when Jesus came to him. And Jesus said to him, "Suffer it now for thus it becometh us to fulfill all righteousness." In other words, the baptism of the water is fine, too. It means the cleansing first. So both are good.

But what did Jesus mean here in detail? The

illumined intellect in you, represented by John, had a very real task in preparing you to receive the Christ or the Deeper Self. You are illumined enough to know that it is there. Now you want to ask yourself, "How illumined is my intellect to receive this Deeper Self and its heaven? There is a considerable task that John performed here as an example of the ILLUMINED INTELLECT:

First, the illumined intellect declares the kingdom is at hand. At least it knew that heaven was not up somewhere in the sky. Then Jesus said, "The Kingdom of Heaven is within you." Have you got that clear? We are just going over fundamentals here, but they are important!

Then the illumined intellect counsels repentance. Does your intellect really see the need for the change? So that you are going to drop your substantiation and support of old conditions you do not want. Mentally turn your back on them. Renounce them. No longer make a big thing out of them. Stop giving yourself to them.

Illumined intellect also recommends purifying the mind by means of denials. Of course, people with Truth background recognize the tendency to say, "I don't even bother with denials anymore. I am only interested in Truth now—the positive things. So I don't bother with denials anymore." Yet the same person, though he comes to church regularly and is advanced supposedly, is always saying when discussions come up, "You know, whenever I overwork a little bit or strain a little bit, I always come down with. . . ." And he names it emphatically. So he still needs to do a little denying, after all.

Whatever you say about yourself—if you believe it—you demonstrate it! You know, some of the things you say about yourself—if somebody else said them, you would not like it even a little bit. Thus those are some of the things to deny. So the next time you open your "big mouth" (that is just an idiom), remember in its place to say to yourself, "Fermez la bouche" or "Shut your mouth." Do not make a big thing out of it. Take it easy. Just stop. Some people think that by denials you have to investigate yourself in depth. Go down into the basement of your subconscious. See all the things that are wrong. And deny them one by one. No, that is just a good way to find more trouble!

The easy way is—when it comes up quite naturally by habit—and you find yourself still saying something you know in Truth you should not—just "fermez la bouche" it. Yes, stop it dead in its tracks. That is all.

Finally illumined intellect causes you to turn and let in the Christ ideas—the ideas of the Deeper Self—God with you.

Now these are the assets of the illumined intellect. We have been considering John The Baptist. That his illumined intellect purifies, cleanses and so forth. Prepares us for something better. But what are its liabilities? Well, its liabilities rest in its tendency just to fight evil. While it is noble in itself just to fight evil, it represents a limited perspective of life when it tends to make an obsession of evil. This was John's fault—his weakness. Would any of that be in you? You want to get rid of something. So you make such a big issue of it; it is such a great challenge. This can lead to being overcome by the very thing you would fight.

This, of course, was symbolized by John, for he finally was imprisoned and beheaded by the very forces of which he was trying to rid himself. When I was very young, I did the same thing—but in a small way. Trying to learn to ride a bicycle for the first time, I found myself headed for a huge tree. Not being able to balance myself properly and steer at the same time, all I could think of and say to myself was, "Whatever you do, don't hit that tree." What do you think happened? I hit it dead center.

"Jesus The Christ" represents, "I am come that they might have life, and that they might have it more abundantly." Jesus rounds out our perspective here, and symbolizes the other half of our subject. He said, "Be not overcome of evil"—the thing that is limited in your life, which you are making too big—"but overcome evil with good."

So, finally, you must learn to overcome your evil with good, and Jesus' application represents this in you. Now the first stage of the spiritual maturing of the Christ in you or the Deeper Self is symbolized by Jesus' announcement at twelve dedicating his life, "Wist ye not that I must be about my Father's business?"

Thus there first must be an announcement to each and every challenge—of that which Jesus did, "Wist ye not that I must be about my Father's business?"

Next, there must be the proper follow through of Truth. And the application given by Jesus was, ". . . whosoever shall smite you on the right cheek, turn to him the other also."

This great technique is badly misunderstood by most people in religion. They think it means that you simply lie down and take a beating. As someone said to me, "You know, I am trying to practice that—'Whosoever shall smite me on one cheek, I will turn to him the other.' But is there such a thing as feeling like a doormat when you do this?"

And I said, "If you feel like a doormat—you are a doormat. You have missed the whole point. It does not mean what you are thinking at all. It means this: Turn from the outer attack —to the Christ in you, the I AM, Jehovah God, this Deeper Self—your hope of glory. And wholeheartedly know that this Deeper Self is releasing the LIVING ACTION of God Himself

in and through you. That it is correcting the
negative thing in you which is attracting the
trouble. That it is also correcting the negative
thing in your adversary which is motivating
his outer actions. That nothing can withstand
the pressure of His Holy Spirit bringing about
the needed order and harmony.

All of which is maturing the Deeper Self
within you!

Spiritual Meditation

"John The Baptist" formed the connecting
link between Judaism and Christianity by his
recognition of Jesus as the Messiah—long promised by a portion of Hebrew prophecy. John
represents ILLUMINED INTELLECT turned
toward spiritual things. It has a four-fold task in
preparing your consciousness to receive the
Christ or your Deeper Self. (1) It believes the
kingdom is at hand. (2) It counsels repentance.
(3) It purifies the mind by means of denials. (4)
It causes you to anticipate the greater—Christ
ideas. These are its assets. Its liabilities lie in its
belief in evil as a reality. Just fighting evil leads
to your imprisonment by the thing you fight.

John in prison, and eventually beheaded, symbolizes that.

The first stage of your spiritual maturity, after your Second Birth, is symbolized by Jesus' announcement of His dedication to God's service at the age of twelve. . . . "Wist ye not that I must be about my Father's business?" "Jesus The Christ" represents, "I am come that they might have life, and that they might have it more abundantly." This is to be attained by— "overcoming evil with good." Thus He symbolizes affirming and establishing the "Truth that sets free" in the face of every challenge. Turning from the outer attack of evil to, "Christ in you, the hope of glory." And knowing wholeheartedly that it is the LIVING ACTION of God, which will overcome this evil with its good. Remember, nothing can withstand the pressure of God's Holy Spirit (this living action) when it is properly released through you.

NEW TESTAMENT

PART III.

"KEYS TO THE KINGDOM"

". . . Behold, there went out a sower to sow:
. . . Some fell by the way side, . . . Some fell on
stony ground . . . Some fell among thorns, . . .
And others fell on good ground, . . ."
Mark 4:3–8

". . . So is the Kingdom of God, as if a man
should cast seed into the ground; . . . For the
earth bringeth forth fruit of herself; first the
blade, then the ear, after that the full corn in
the ear."   Mark 4:26–28

"The kingdom of heaven is like unto leaven,
which a woman took, and hid in three measures of meal, till the whole was leavened."
Matthew 13:33

"Again, the kingdom of heaven is like unto
treasure hid in a field; the which when a man
hath found, he hideth, and for joy thereof
goeth and selleth all that he hath, and buyeth
that field."   Matthew 13:44

206

"Again, the kingdom of heaven is like unto a merchant man, seeking goodly pearls: Who, when he had found one pearl of great price, went and sold all that he had, and bought it."
Matthew 13:45, 46

"Again, the kingdom of heaven is like unto a net, that was cast into the sea, and gathered of every kind: Which, when it was full, they drew to shore, and sat down, and gathered the good into vessels, but cast the bad away."
Matthew 13:47, 48

This segment has to do with our subject, "Keys to The Kingdom," as given in the Bible. And the whole of it is done in parables. This is a Jewish mode of teaching, which was practiced by Jesus in particular—teaching in parables. Strangely enough it is the nearest thing to metaphysics. Because it is taking something you know, an incident of life, something with which you are very familiar—and through it, being made to see a very great Truth. In a way, that is what metaphysics does. It gets behind the scene to what counts.

Now we are about to do some of these parables. I will do as many as we have room for, but I want to "milk" each one for its full value to you. To emphasize how great they are, here is a preface of Biblical passages, which you do not have listed at the outset of this segment. If you would like to know the location, it is Matthew 13, verses 34 and 35. Here is given the grandeur of these parables in advance:

"All these things spake Jesus unto the multitude in parables: . . . That it might be fulfilled which was spoken by the prophet, saying, I will open my mouth in parables. I will utter things which have been kept secret from the foundation of the world." This is what you are about to receive.

During the second year of His ministry Jesus gave nine keys to the kingdom of heaven by means of parables. Now this man is the dominant figure of the New Testament. We have just as carefully considered Moses of the Old Testament, as well as Abraham, Jacob and Joseph. We are seeking now to find the main value—the dominant figure of the New Testament has to our own lives.

Jesus taught deep Truths through these parables, and we need to understand that a parable is a short fictitious story based upon a familiar experience. Having a specific application to our spiritual life, it unlocks something that we may miss. Now the parable was a favorite Jewish mode of teaching. In Jesus' hands He imparted to it the richest and most perfect development. So often he took an incident common to everyday life to set forth a great spiritual Truth. And we are going to consider now as many as we have room for in this book.

To Peter, Jesus began the "Keys to The Kingdom" in parable form, when He said, "Whatsoever thou shalt bind on earth shall be bound in heaven: and whatsoever thou shalt loose on earth shall be loosed in heaven." Our parable here is making this great point: People have the tendency to attach themselves to negative things in their earth—their privately experienced world—exactly as they factually exist. Such people are binding and limiting their ideas to those hard, material conditions. They take their idea from the fact, and then live with that fact. And what is "bound on earth" is "bound in heaven." Thus, they become slaves to that which they really do not want.

Those, on the other hand, who look right

through the apparent hardship of earthly environment that may be around them. Persistently declare themselves not bound to that state. Are persons, who—"having found the Spirit of God, walk with that Spirit." They "see what the Father is doing" there. That becomes their idea. When they have determined this, then they totally become that mentally or "go and do likewise." This brings the miracle!

So the challenge to you here is to stop binding yourself to any lack under which you may be suffering—any sickness, injustice, pain or inharmony. Stop binding it on earth and loose its opposite from God.

Now let me illustrate so that you see it very clearly. What would you think of a so-called student of Truth who was constantly changing practitioners? The person names factual conditions in her body, in her human relations and in her business. Tells the practitioner what she would like to see happen in each.

This is an actual case. It is not anyone you would ever know. But it could be anyone of us where we are. She sets the practitioner to working these three conditions out. She must have come from the old school where you would keep a little clock or watch to see how long it takes the practitioner to demonstrate for you. When contacted by her practitioner she immediately says, "Are you sure you are working? Because the body hasn't changed, the human relations are still a mess and business could be ever so much better." She stays with that practitioner a little while. Then finally calls up and says, "Please don't treat for me any more. Things are getting worse than they used to be."

So she gets another practitioner, and names the three factual cases in her life again. Tells him exactly what she would like to see happen in each case, and to get to work immediately on it. Then every time he contacts her she says, "You're sure you are working? I just let go of another practitioner, you know. Nothing happened. He didn't work. So be sure you are working on this." Pretty soon she phones and says, "Don't treat anymore. Things are getting worse. Got to get another practitioner."

The study of Truth is not realized through having a practitioner live your life for you. If you do that, the only thing I can say for you is that you have given your practitioner plenty of exercise in Truth. All of which is nice of you. But you yourself are still plenty flabby, because you have not done anything. There has been no exercise of Truth in you. However, this is not to say there are never times when the individual needs a practitioner to help him through something.

But in the particular type case I have described in detail, the person is almost daring any practitioner to work a miracle. It is as though that person takes pride in saying, "No one can help me. I'm real special." Do you begin to see this? The person says she wants her challenges worked out. But is doing everything to keep it from happening. Why? Because she is gluing her mind on the hard conditions in her life. Not doing one blessed thing to change her mind from these things. At best, only hoping the practitioner will get favorable results. Here again, we are witnessing a person really "binding" herself to hard conditions in her life.

With every challenge you must change your idea from the way the picture factually is to what the Father is doing in your behalf. The same as the practitioner must do. Yes, really get hold of what God wants done there. Live and walk with that idea. Then there is nothing in the human behavior pattern of the world that can stop the Grace or Higher Action of God from producing its new phenomenon in your life. Please think about that!

Here is the next parable. I want to get to the heart of it in any way that comes to me. It is the Parable of the Sower. We already know something about it, I suppose, from somewhere along the line of our study—so we will review it just briefly. It teaches us that "The Sower," which is the indwelling Christ or the Deeper Self, is always speaking the Word of Truth outward from the deep within of us—to our subconscious. Do you get that picture at all? Yes, "the Sower," in the Parable of The Sower, is the Christ or Deeper Self of you, and it is always speaking the Truth to your subconscious.

You see, God does not change. And the Christ or the Deeper Self of us—is His individualized Presence in us. In the beginning, God created us in such a way as to be able to operate directly upon our subconscious or feeling nature. From there up to the canvas of our conscious mind or knowing nature, and thence out into the world. Causing us to be His manifesting nature or what He wants done—and thus come off at our best. While God does not deviate from His original plan of working thorugh us, He also gave us free will or freedom of choice. And in choosing the outer or way of the world—then as well as now —we lost and continue to lose our way. In religious circles this is known as, "The Fall of Man."

Now in the study of Truth today we are getting back to God. And it is interesting to note that regardless of where we are in unfoldment, the plan still remains. The Christ, the Deeper Self, God's individualized Presence in us—is constantly speaking His Word of Truth to our subconscious. Thus it only remains how much asleep we are or how dead we are in consciousness to His Word. The whole of Truth is to wake up our subconscious. Make it responsive again to God. Get back to the original plan.

In the meantime, there are four types of hearers of that Truth. Four levels of being asleep, dead, in between, or awake. In enumerating them quickly, the whole point is to ask yourself which of these YOU ARE at your present level of unfoldment.

With the first type of hearer—this Word—from the Christ or Deeper Self speaking to his subconscious or feeling nature ". . . falls by the wayside" and ". . . the birds devour them," the Bible tells us. Meaning that spiritual understanding is utterly lacking in this type of hearer. Sense consciousness in him, to which he totally gives himself, quickly obliterates whatever the Christ or Deeper Self is trying to implant in him. That is self explanatory, is it not? He is so lost in sense consciousness that nothing from God "takes." He is one of those who, if he ever turns God's way, says, "Oh God, if there is a God, help my soul, if I have a soul." And goes wandering on in life.

The second type of hearer is a most interesting one. He is different. He gladly receives the Word—in church or anywhere else. But he owns only a surface consciousness or rocky soil. "Rocky places," as the Bible puts it. Meaning, that when trials come, he thrusts the Word aside. He does not really use it. Because he does not really believe it. He wants to, but his is a sense consciousness, too. Delightful person, but there is no real spiritual development in him.

Let me illustrate: I have never forgotten this

gentleman, whom I met in Boston many years ago. He was most charming, a delightful person in every way. But what stands out about him most in my memory is this: I would meet him for two Sundays in a row. After each service, he would impress me so much. His reactions were so vital. He would say, "My heavens, these people are not awake. How can they hear this without just going out and throwing their hats in the air! It is marvelous! And the things I am going to do." Then, the next time I would see him, after the second Sunday, would be about eight months later. He would come in with the same enthusiastic approach. "You remember me, don't you? My, that Truth is wonderful. I really count myself fortunate to be here today, and so forth." When would I see him again? In about two years. Do you get the point?

The third type of hearer intrigues my imagination. His mind wants to hear the Word, but his consciousness is like "thorny ground." Because this is the way he lives. He hears the Word for his healing, for every side of his life—what God wants done there. But his is a "thorny consciousness." The majority of his consciousness is identified or obsessed with burdens in the forms of the cares of the world. He is ladened down with them. No Truth student should be guilty of putting his head in the sand. But this fellow just glues himself to television, the all-news programs. Can hardly wait for the next one, which is simply a repeat of the one he has just heard. Loves to get it all. He is burdened down with it, you see. Also he is burdened down with the deceitfulness of the world. If you have time, he will tell you just how deceitful it is. This is his consciousness. So it is a "thorny consciousness." He hears the Word, but he is too taken up with the woes of the world.

Do you remember that old story I love so much? Sam wanted to change the whole world, and people just were not doing anything about it. They would hear, they would see—but do nothing. So he decided to do the whole thing himself. Before going to bed that night, he really got himself all worked up. Prayed and prayed far into the night. Fists clenched, sweat coming down his brow, he was going all out for the whole world. To remove all the wickedness, all the trouble everywhere. Half way through the night, God's voice spoke to him, "Sam, go to bed. I'll take it the rest of the way."

Some people, you see, under the guise of God —are only practicing humanism. Humanism is good and is needed. But will never produce a miracle. You have to reach the place in mind where you represent a Being greater than yourself. Get this straight. Moses was nothing until he represented something greater than himself. Jacob was nothing until he became Israel. Meaning at-one-ment with a Being greater than himself. Abraham was nothing until he went with the covenant from a Being greater than himself. Joseph was the same. Jesus never healed, prospered or harmonized anyone of Himself, but only through the Christ—the individualization of Someone greater, even the Father within. Remember that!

Now let us consider the fourth type of hearer. "The Sower" sows and finds good ground. This is one who, through the study of Truth or a natural love of God, is really fertile soil. So the Word of God is able to bring its seed to abundant harvest through this person. That is what happened to Abraham, Isaac, Jacob, Joseph, Moses and Jesus. Of themselves they did not do it. A Being greater than they overwhelmed them, and became them—in the working out of a problem.

If you are one of those who says, "Oh, no. I do it all myself. That's all there is. Let's face it. This is practical, and this is real." No! This is foolishness. That is not the answer. You could never replace your God. In that sense Jesus knew, "One is greater than I, even the Father." This Great Creative Spirit is everywhere equally present. You can go great distances both physically and mentally. But God would already be there before you arrived. You are still just this individualization. The best you can do is express Him in the places you go. The great wayshowers of the Old and New Testaments alike were "good soil," because they knew a God greater than themselves. This they became. Then they were "gods," yes—but with a little "g." They were still only His manifesting nature.

So it is then, that we have set up these four types of hearers of the Word of God as was given in the Bible—for the purpose of you asking yourself where you are as a hearer.

The Parable of The Growing Seed is something else. It is very interesting, because it teaches that our consciousness develops in the same mysterious way that seeds do—with any Truth that we want to make manifest. Like the next goal you have in mind. As the Bible puts it, "By their fruits ye shall know them." Should it come to pass, it means you have been left on higher ground. It means God was able to get through you into expression. We would all like to speak the Word, and the thing of God be done instantly. But we do not start there. Very much like a seed—this does not usually happen overnight. Rather, "First the blade, then the ear, and then the full grain in the ear." That is the way a seed progresses, and that is the way your demonstration progresses through you.

We do not generally reap a full harvest as soon as the seed is planted or sown. You are sowing the seed at the start of any period of spiritual treatment toward a goal. This great period concentrates your attention to the point of working with God in a realistic way. Therefore, remain patient and faithful. Gently insist upon the working out of your next goal. Have a growing sense of joy about it because it is in the process of working out. Soon you should be surfeited with joy, full of it, anticipating what is going to happen. And it will!

Now the Parable of The Leaven is something we all say we already know. The question is, do we? It teaches that we must put the Word of Truth into a condition in our lives. Just like leaven must be put into bread if it is to be fit to eat. So it is, that if you do not like the condition facing you in your life, it, too, is not fit for you. It also needs the leaven of the Word of God put into it. The Word works invisibly and silently. Even though we may think there is no progress, much progress is being made. In due time a substantial and beneficial change for the better in the outer will take place, if we let this invisible, silent work keep right on doing its job—the invisible, silent work of the Word!

The Parable of The Hidden Treasure is also an interesting one. It makes us to realize that even though we may discover Truth quite unexpectedly, we do not own it until we have paid the necessary price for it. A good way to start a conversation in this field is to say, "How did you happen to get started in Truth?" Then the other person says, "Well, in my case I sort of stumbled on it." Or, "I got hold of a set of books in the library, and it confirmed something I always felt." Or, "A friend said this had helped him.

He wasn't pushing anything on me, but this had really worked for him. He simply told his story, and it appealed to me." So it does seem as though Truth came into our lives unexpectedly. But not really. If we were not somehow ready, it would not have "taken."

However, eventually we must pay the full price for this study of Truth in which we find ourselves. That is, if we are to have its full benefits. The cost lies in surrendering to Truth the necessary time, devotion and obedience. We must finally look upon Truth as the greatest thing in our lives, because it has the capacity to make all other things great.

Now the "treasure hid in the field" may be something that you do not understand as it is given in the Bible, because Jesus used something here that was commonplace ONLY in His day. You see, in His day they did not have any banks. So the practice was, if you had a plot of ground, you dug a hole and put your savings in it. Now because many people did this, it had to happen that some of those holes were forgotten through death and left untouched. Years later, someone would find one by seeming chance. This happened so many times, they had to make a law.

The law was you had to buy the land, where you found the treasure, in order to claim it. Interesting?

The parable is saying the same now about your "hidden treasure." Like those who found the "treasure hid in the field," long ago, you today must go out and "sell everything you have" as they did, in order to own this greatest of all treasures, the "Truth that sets free."

We can only hope that the treasure found by those dear ones long ago was equal to what they gave away in order to buy the plot of ground. But the "hidden treasure" in you is something else. It should be first in your life because it changes everything else in your life for the better. Now unless you believe that, you are not really in Truth. Yes, unless you believe Truth to be the "hidden treasure" of your life, and that through it, everything else can be changed dramatically for the better. If you are just lackadaisical about the point I have just made, you are not with it yet. You do not grasp it yet. As they say in today's parlance, "You don't dig it yet." It must be first, then it changes everything else. Until you see that—you are lacking in consciousness for its entrance into your world!

The Pearl of Great Price, another parable, cites the same great point. It is trying to teach us that we must be like the merchant in gems, who was seeking all his life for the pearl of great price. For this he would do everything. He would sell everything he had to get it. He made a fetish of the finest gem it would be possible to find. This, too, must be our criterion—a whole-hearted persistence for the pearl of great price, which is Truth. Once we have that doggedness, we will find that God is our ultimate good in every issue of our lives. He will prove Himself to be the answer.

The Parable of The Net also fascinates me a great deal. Because if you stop to think about it, your mind is a net that has been cast into the sea of universal life. And when we come into spiritual understanding, only the ideas that increase our spiritual stature will be preserved. Yes, our mind is like a net that we throw out into the world and into the within. We gather into the net as the fishermen did years and years ago. Even as they looked in the net, after they drew it in, and took the good that they found and threw the rest away—so must we!

Are you going to sharpen your mind to that?

Or are you still going to take everything that comes into the net and gobble it down—good, bad and indifferent? You live in a dual world of good and bad. Face it! Therefore you must reach the place where you understand the difference between receiving something and accepting something. You cannot help receiving both good and bad. You cannot avoid getting a mixture from the world all the time, through television, radio, everything. No, you simply cannot help receiving both, but you alone determine that which you accept! Whatever you bring into your net, stay with that which makes for Truth and accept only it. To the rest just say, "Sorry, I'm not doing business with you any more." That is correct living!

Now I will close with this. The phrase, "the end of the world," was used in two of the nine parables of Jesus. "The end of the world" does not mean the physical dissolution of the earth, but the end of a particular phase in your experience. We all want our next goal worked out. If we ask for guidance from God—and that is what we have been doing in our spiritual treatment periods about that goal—He will overcome the vicious, destructive beliefs of the race. Cast into the furnace all that has held us back.

So there will be considerable "weeping and gnashing of teeth" on the part of the destructive beliefs of the race that have held us in their spell.

Yes, they will be "weeping and gnashing their teeth" over having to leave you. They do not give up easily. They do not want to relinquish their hold on you. They would like to keep you down to their level—these destructive beliefs of the race. But now there will be an end to that hold—an end to that world. In its place will now come the fulfillment of this promise, "Behold, I will do a new thing; now it shall spring forth; shall ye not know it?" Why? Because you will LET IT—by remaining steadfast and wholehearted in your expectancy Godward!

Spiritual Meditation

During the second year of His ministry, Jesus gave nine keys to the kingdom of heaven by means of parables. A parable is a short, fictitious narrative based on a familiar experience and having an application to spiritual life. The parable was a favorite Jewish mode of teaching, and Jesus imparted to it the richest and most perfect development. Invariably Jesus took an incident from everyday life to set forth a spiritual Truth.

To Peter (faith) Jesus began the keys to the kingdom of heaven in parable form when He said, "Whatsoever thou shalt bind on earth shall be bound in heaven: and whatsoever thou shalt loose on earth shall be loosed in heaven."

Persons, who let their thinking attach itself to negative things in their earth (privately expressed world) exactly as they factually exist, are binding and limiting their ideas to those hard, material conditions. Thereby, they are becoming slaves to what they really do not want.

Those, who look right through the apparent hardships of earthly environments, and persistently declare themselves not bound to that status—are persons, who, "having found the Spirit of God, walk in that Spirit." They "see what the Father is doing" there, and become that totally in their mentalities or "go and do likewise" what they have seen the Father doing.

So the challenge to you here is STOP binding your poverty, sickness, obstacles, injustices and inharmonies on earth—and LOOSE their opposites from God—what you belong to there in Him!

Yes, "See what the Father is doing" . . . and "go and do likewise."

John 5:19

NEW TESTAMENT

PART IV.

"THE SERMON ON THE MOUNT
OR
THE BEATITUDES"

Blessed are the poor in spirit: for theirs is the kingdom of heaven."

"Blessed are they that mourn: for they shall be comforted."

"Blessed are the meek: for they shall inherit the earth."

"Blessed are they which do hunger and thirst after righteousness: for they shall be filled."

"Blessed are the merciful: for they shall obtain mercy."

"Blessed are the pure in heart: for they shall see God."

"Blessed are the peacemakers: for they shall be called the Children of God."

"Blessed are they which are persecuted for righteousness' sake: for theirs is the kingdom of heaven."

"Blessed are ye, when men shall revile you, and persecute you, and shall say all manner of evil against you falsely, for My sake."

"Rejoice, and be exceeding glad: for great is
your reward in heaven: for so persecuted they
the prophets which were before you."

Matthew 5:3 thru 12

Our subject is, The Sermon On The Mount,
which has as its other name, The Beatitudes.
Just as The Decalogue is another name for the
revered Ten Commandments. Strangely enough,
The Sermon On The Mount and The Ten Commandments go together, and bring you something extremely viable for all time.

Now let us see how important this material is.
Remember, the second title of this segment has
to do with right attitudes. The title is saying,
"Be these attitudes."

We often hear the remark, "He is well meaning, a good fellow and all; but he has the wrong
attitude." Of course, no one ever says that about
you, but you have known such people.

It is strange about life. You can have ability.
Have the capacity for "wearing out the seat of
your pants," as they say in business—which

means remaining steadfast on a job until you get it done. Yes, you can have all that kind of equipment, but still open your mouth and express an attitude—which is holding you back. What is really being said is that you have the wrong spirit.

Yes, whenever it is said a person has a wrong attitude—that this is holding him back. What is really being said is that he has the wrong spirit. How did he happen to get that way? Well, no one knows, but he picked it up from somewhere. What is it? It is a cluster of negative ideas under which he labors.

These ideas have bred his spirit or his attitude. Since his spirit or attitude is his feeling, and he only demonstrates what he feels—no matter how hard he works, he holds himself back. Until he breaks his attitude, or it breaks him.

Hundreds of books in psychology have been written on how to get the right attitude. And I am sure they have not hurt. Rather have been helpful. But the greatest resumé of perfect attitudes is found in this segment. Once again—

that is why it is called, THE BE-ATTITUDES. I have given this brief preface to make you realize the possibilities that lie within this subject. Weigh these perfect attitudes in terms of your own. Wherever you may fall short, it is nobody's business but your own. However, you may well find just the right answers to your needs, and so correct them.

The Decalogue or The Ten Commandments and The Beatitudes or The Sermon on The Mount are similar, in that both represent the Higher Law of God.

It was a great day in the history of man when Higher Law was first revealed. That came through Moses and The Ten Commandments. He brought into play the understanding that God is not a God of whimsy. That He operates by Law. That if you pass the conditions of response to God, He has to operate in an exact way. Higher Law merely means that exact way in which He would operate in your life or the plan of God for man.

The only thing you and I really suffer from is lower law, meaning limited beliefs that we have picked up from the outer. When you have picked up a negative belief from the race, and you really believe that way; it becomes a law to your consciousness. The wonderful thing to know here is that you do not have to settle for that. It is beneath you. You do not belong to it. You can break through. You can repeal it. You can still come under Higher Law, the Plan of God for you. And Moses, through great inspiration, brought the first pronouncement of God as Law.

Now in The Sermon on The Mount we have this to consider: It is not different from The Ten Commandments in its content substancewise. Yet they are different in the sense that The Decalogue or The Ten Commandments was a stern delineation of right and wrong. In The Sermon on The Mount or The Beatitudes, the same pronouncement of the Higher Law of God is given. But the stern delineation of right and wrong is mitigated to a passionate appeal for right thinking in you, and thereby right feeling or the right attitude.

Let us understand the apparent difference. One presents the Law in terms of, "Thou shalt not." No "ifs" or "buts" about it. It is stated sharply. The other tells you that your life will be a blessed one, if you attain certain spiritual attitudes. The difference in presentation in each instance was right for the times. Because it was in keeping with what man was intellectually and emotionally ready to receive.

Let us have a deep appreciation of the time in which The Ten Commandments or The Decalogue was given. These dear people had come out of abject slavery over a long period. They wandered around for forty years before they entered their Promised Land. The distance, however, could not have been further than from New York City to Buffalo, New York. Purposely Moses caused the trip to be done very slowly for one reason—rehabilitation. Being in abject slavery is something that we know about best through experience. Then only can we fully conceive of the degradation involved. Even when Moses came down from Mount Sinai, you will remember—his people had gone back to worshipping idols. Something they could see. That should give you some idea of the state in which they were. After long years of slavery, they had become rather primitive.

So the Law, found in The Ten Commandments or The Decalogue, the Higher Law of God, had to be couched in firm language. "Thou shalt not . . ." was a wonderful presentation for them. Actually it makes up the civil laws for most of the civilized world even today. Such is still couched in a language for the primitive. For those, who as yet have to be imprisoned for a while, and so forth. I have taken the time here to make you see why it had to be done. Yes, to help people at a very primitive level long ago. And to help primitive people still today who need that kind of presentation.

In the same sense we have religions today, you know, that present their beliefs in strong language. Their main forte is to "scare the hell" out of people. And I am not being profane here. However, there are millions of people today, who long since have no need for that kind of presentation. They are ready to seek God— because of the fruits that belong to them, and which can be theirs.

What I am emphasizing through these opening remarks, then, is that The Sermon on The Mount in no sense of the word is intended to abrogate the revered Ten Commandments. They were the first pronouncements of the Higher Law of God. Rather, The Sermon on The Mount has been given us to teach us how to fulfill the same Law in the complete, spiritual sense—meaning through love.

Love is the highest fulfillment of the Law. Yes, when you love to do it. Each of the statements in The Beatitudes, pointedly makes clear to our understanding, that there is always a condition to be passed before the fruit can be enjoyed by our person. And the condition named in each of the eight Beatitudes is an attitude of loving the Higher Law.

In other words, in every instance there has to be a certain attitude in us before we can enjoy the state of being, which is its fruit. We have to be the attitude first. Again, that is what beatitude means. We are now going to consider this condition in each of The Beatitudes, and the fruit that can be ours. Yes, we are going to consider the attitude we must garner unto ourselves in order to have the wonderful state of being that it produces.

The First Statement of Higher Law in The Beatitudes tells us, "Blessed are the poor in spirit, for theirs is the kingdom of heaven." Now I have been showing you all through the parables, the allegories and the historical sections of the Bible, that you must always relate their inner meaning to your personal life. The same with Bible promises, you must always look for the polar words or phrases and relate them to yourself in order to get the real "meat" of the promise. You must also remember that the Bible, written so many years ago, is in a kind of archaic language. So some of the terms may have to be deciphered.

For example, "poor in spirit" does not have the connotation you might ascribe to it. In those days what it was saying is this: "Poor in spirit" is the condition you must pass. But the intended meaning of the condition is that we be sufficiently humble or teachable so that we are willing and eager to relinquish our limited human concept for the higher concept of God. "Sackcloth and ashes," or pretended humility, will not do. We must come front and center with what is required.

Real humility is teachableness. Are you teachable? Are you open to a change in ideas? So that your attitude or feeling about that particular side of life can change also. That is what the promise is saying. To paraphrase, "Blessed are those humble enough, teachable enough, to take on corrective ideas from God, so that their attitude will be different." The point is all too clear. Are you willing to learn from God? Are you willing to listen to His Words? Are you willing to follow them, believing that this is the higher way to the "life more abundant?"

Now, if you are willing, there is a fruit promised to you: "Theirs is the kingdom of heaven." Yes, you will own that much more of the kingdom of heaven. Even though that kingdom is within you—if you are not open, it may as well be over Australia. Of course, some people are happy to have it up somewhere on the Milky Way. Never think of letting any of it happen in their earth this time around.

Strange thing, no one has ever figured out how the kingdom of heaven got up there somewhere on the Milky Way.

I sometimes think it has been a safe place to put it, so that one can go on with his own way of life down here. But the man who knew the most about it, Jesus, said, "The kingdom of heaven is within you." And there is no way you can honestly twist that!

How teachable are you? The fruit is that you will have that much of the kingdom of heaven.

Now let us consider this: Once we have passed the condition of being humble or teachable Godward, inevitably our minds must develop spiritually—until we come to the realization of omnipresent substance. Yes, God being everywhere equally present, His substance must be the same. This means that there is a life-substance or "know how" from God for your body that always wants to come in to make it better. That there is a love substance or "know how" from God that wants to come in to and enable you to go on growing, expanding and enjoying greater human relations. That there is a prospering substance or "know how" from God, peculiar to business, that wants to come in and take you to sure success and supply sufficient and to spare.

The only thing standing in the way would be a know-it-all attitude. Such as, "After all I have been to college. I know the sciences, and there is hardly anything in religion that could offer me more." You would be surprised! There is a "know how" you will never get in the greatest universities. A "know how" of life for your body. A "know how" of love for your human relations. A "know how" of prosperity and success for your business—when you are ready!

Now the Second Statement of Higher Law in The Beatitudes tells us, "Blessed are they that mourn, for they shall be comforted." Once again, you must understand the language. "Mourning," spiritually utilized, is the condition here. If you mourn in the right way, you pass the condition. Life is not all joy. Much of our greatest unfoldment has come through a mourning period. The key to this is found in an old adage, "Man's extremity is God's opportunity." You have heard of that. Well, we need to utilize it.

What it is saying here is this: Let the trials and tribulations, which cause you to mourn, now cause you to do something other than just mourn. In your mourning, turn to God! Do not just mourn. Let any mourning, that you may do, turn you to Him. That is the condition. "They shall be comforted," is the fruit. If you mourn in the right way, if it is utilized spiritually, you will be comforted. That is the fruit.

The condition again is "mourning that turns you to God." Yes, once your attitude has become this. Then you have found the silver lining to the cloud. There shall be, paraphrasing the Bible, "Beauty for ashes, and the oil of joy for all this mourning." You will be helped, you will be comforted. So always remember, when you have a tendency to mourn, do not waste it. Let it turn you to God. That you may be comforted in a way no one else can provide.

The Third Statement of Higher Law in The Beatitudes tells us, "Blessed are the meek, for they shall inherit the earth." You would be surprised at the connotations attached to that. Some people react to the statement this way to use today's parlance, "Well that means the worst "drips" in the world—in the end get it all." This is usually said by someone who is quite certain he is not a "drip." The real meaning has no relation to that. "Blessed are the meek: for they shall inherit the earth," means that meekness is the condition. That it is something we need to develop. That it is a condition not to be passed up in our spiritual unfoldment.

The true understanding of "meekness" is this: It means a willingness on our part to do God's will. You know, we all have a tendency to be a little "bullheaded," to use today's parlance again. We want it our way. We need to learn to surrender our will to God's will. But not from the old theological view. In the old theological view, it was always used when you did not understand something. And in the old theological view, God's view was never very good or nice. It was usually something you had to take, and then make the best of a bad bargain.

Now you have to get that out of your system. Because it simply has never been true.

Meekness means spiritual willingness. It is an art to learn. The surrendering of your own will to God. It is something you would want to work for, when you understand that the will of God is the greatest thing that could ever happen to you in any instant in eternity. Always remember that. It wipes out all the old-time theology that was wrong. Yes, God's will is always the greatest thing that could ever happen to you in any instant in eternity. In nearly all cases it is nine times better than your best. Once in a while your best is "on the beam." But then it is completely in tune with His will. Most of the time His way is so much better. Never is it less!

If you can burn that into your brain, you have learned a great deal.

"They shall inherit the earth," is the fruit here. Yes, "Blessed are the meek for they shall inherit the earth." You are acquainted with the Lord's Prayer, where it says, "Thy kingdom come. Thy will be done in earth, as it is in heaven." Think of that, your earth as it is in heaven. This is what you want!

Let me help you here. I tell you honestly, I work towards goals—very definite goals. The best I can see for myself. But always with this aside, "Either this, or that which in God's sight is better." Yet it never deters me from going all out toward those goals to the best of my ability, because I have allowed for the possibility of a surprise-package ending. Better than what I may think. And I always like that.

Once we get onto this, we truly "inherit the earth." Because our earth—our body, business and human relations—begins more and more to take on expression as God would have it. If we are willing to do His will, then His will happens —nearly always better than our best. And this is what we are after. One of the finest ways of finding out that we have dominion over all external conditions is when we finally learn— this meekness!

Now the Fourth Statement of Higher Law in The Beatitudes tells us, "Blessed are they that hunger and thirst after righteousness: for they shall be filled." It means what? On the surface it sounds like a "goody-two-shoes" phrase. So you just read it and turn the page. Had enough of that already. "There are enough 'Holy Joes' now," you say.

But it does not mean that at all. "Hunger and thirst after righteousness" is the condition here.

"Righteousness" merely means the right or spiritual use of our physical, mental and spiritual faculties. This is what we are all really after. I think everyone is seeking—whatever his way of religion may be—to find out how to be himself. That is all.

What we are after here—to pass the condition then—is a passion for really finding out how to be ourselves. Right physically. Right mentally. Right spiritually. That passion is personally hungering and thirsting after righteousness. The fruit for such people is that they shall be filled with this "right-use-ness" for their persons. Yes, when your attitude Godward is a passion. When you take a delight in finding the right use of yourself. Then you have totally passed the condition and deserve the fruit. Yes, "Delight thyself also in the Lord;" (the Higher Law) "and He shall give thee the desires of thine heart." (Psalm 37:4) When you seek because you are delighted in doing it, not because "you ought to" or "it can't do any harm," you have arrived; and you are on the spiritual beam with this beatitude!

The Fifth Statement of Higher Law in The

Beatitudes takes us further, "Blessed are the merciful: for they shall obtain (receive) mercy." This is a tender subject. "Merciful" is the condition, which sooner or later we must pass in our spiritual unfoldment. But this attitude, when we have passed it, must be in our hearts. This is simply the way we must feel—not just something we know about in our heads. Going through with a deed of mercy with an inner reluctance to do so—or doing it because we ought to—is not enough. Then, too, we always have the world to influence us here, which certainly does not help. It will say to you if you would be merciful, "Why be kind; others will only take advantage of you?" How many times have you heard that? But when we finally have this mercy in our heart, it is tremendously valuable to our person. For having this mercy in our hearts for others, this is a surety. We ourselves will be cared for more quickly. Why? Because, by our attitude, we are close to God. What was the original statement? "Blessed are the merciful, for they shall obtain (receive) mercy."

I know you try to do everything absolutely right. But, if you should ever go slightly off, would it not be nice to know that you are conditioned for mercy in your case. Thus it is a worthwhile condition in the heart—to be attained. It has been made quite clear here that you always receive mercy in proportion to being merciful. That this is the Law. Once you get that down, you have found new freedom.

Now the Sixth Statement of Higher Law in The Beatitudes tells us, "Blessed are the pure in heart, for they shall see God." People read that and say, "How beautiful," and turn the page. But actually the fruit here to be attained— plays a big role in my book, "Beyond Positive Thinking." The art here is to see what the Father is doing—and then become only that with regard to your problem. Right away a half dozen people will say, "Well, how do you see what the Father is doing?"

First you have to understand that God's will is good—and only good. That His will is ALWAYS WONDERFUL as to what it would do in your body, business, human relations, and so forth—if you would let His will be your will. So the art of being able to see what the Father is doing is important. And being "pure in heart" in order to do that—is vital! Yes, "Blessed are the pure in heart, for they shall see God." Pure in heart, then, is the tremendous condition to be

passed. The Psalmist put it well when he said,
"Create in me a clean heart, O Lord; . . ."
(Psalms 51:10) He knew that impurity in the
spiritual sense implies double vision, seeing
good and evil.

James, another forceful writer in the Bible, is
equally pungent. He did not "pull his punches"
at all. He put it this way. "A double-minded
man is unstable in all his ways." (James 1:8)
Even if such a person were to get to the point of
Truth, where he is able to see what God could
possibly do in his life; he would be so full of
what the world was doing, he would negate it!

Suppose you are trying to sell something. I say
this for myself, as well as for you, because I am
working on something in that vein. Now you
know in Truth that God has provided the right
buyer. So you see that. Then, in committing it
to God, you feel an action going for you that
otherwise you would not have. Next, you do
everything you know to do in the outer, but you
continue to allow this inner action to take place
from God. Finally, you are Truth student
enough to know that this is the technique of the
spiritually intelligent.

Yet in the next breath you say, "Well, I would not live on that street myself, I think it has gone down." Or "We are going through a period where that particular type of housing is not so saleable." Mind you, this is the same Truth student saying that. Now that is double-mindedness. So you are unstable as a channel for God's action.

We have to learn to see what the Father is doing, and that is all we must see. Do you get the single-mindedness of faith here? Pure in heart—"pure" means unmixed then. Free of defilement from what the world says. You could not care less, if you are working with God.

Those whose hearts have reached this stage, they direct their whole attention to God. Their hearts remain pure only to what He is. Thus these people will see God. And what they have seen Him doing from within, with regard to their problem—they will see without. That is the fruit! Yes, they will become mentally what He is doing. Such is the purity of their attitude. They are not defiled by the world. They remain pure in heart. And so the thing of God is able to get through. Thus this beatitude is a very valuable condition to pass in growing up spiritually. So make it part of your attitude!

The Seventh Statement of Higher Law in The Beatitudes tells us, "Blessed are the peacemakers: for they shall be called the Children of God." People read that and say, "How true, but this is not a world where there is very much peace." However, it has to begin with you. Peacemaking is the condition. The peacemakers are persons. Now let us see if you want to belong. The "peacemakers" are persons who make peace outwardly, because they have already attained an inner peace.

Regardless of what is on television, in the newspapers, and so forth—they are at peace with God. They are also at peace with others no matter what their outer traits may be. So they bring peace to all situations in which they are involved. They are never lost in the chaos.

Some people right off say, "You can't put your head in the sand. You have to know what is going on." Yes, you need to know what is going on, but you do not have to become that—

by dwelling on it. You need to know what is going on, but for the purpose of bringing peace. Sometimes the very best way to get started as a peacemaker is to look for points of agreement in any situation. That is a good starting point. Most people always look for the points and things, where they are so far apart nothing could bring them together. So look for points of agreement. Be at peace, and try to share that which makes for agreement. This has to be helpful.

Now the fruit here is that you actually "become an outer Child of God" through this practice. It is one of the very best evidences that you have brought this Divine Self into expression. Because the essence of your person, as God planned it, was what? To bring peace on earth, and good will toward men!

So the fruit you are going to have through passing the condition or taking on the attitude of being a peacemaker is—to paraphrase an old Biblical passage—"Having found the Spirit of God, they that walk by the Spirit—are, for all practical purposes, literally the Sons or Children of God."

The Eighth and Final statement of Higher Law in The Beatitudes tells us, "Blessed are they that are persecuted for righteousness' sake: for theirs is the kingdom of heaven. Blessed are ye when men shall reproach you, persecute you and say vile things about you. Rejoice, and be exceeding glad: for great is your reward in heaven."

For someone whose heaven is up on cloud nine, it seems to say, "Don't worry about the persecution from lesser souls, because of your pursuit of righteousness. The more miserably you are treated here, the greater will be your reward in heaven."

But for the person whose heaven is within— as Jesus knew it to be—the meaning of these passages is something quite different. It is saying, "Great is your reward in the heaven that is right with you."

How could that be? Well, wait a minute! What you are after here is the right spiritual use of your physical, mental and spiritual faculties. That is what everyone is after. He may not describe it that way; but everyone is trying to find himself, so that he may come off at his best. This right-use-ness of life, frankly, is opposed by every negative state of consciousness in the race, and every state of mind in you that is less than it. Remember this, only those who do not come "up to par" would ridicule, reproach, say false things, and persecute that which is "up to par." Why? Because "par" is bigger than they are. Your false habits, false beliefs, wrong ways of living—hate not only you but also these changes for the better you would make. This falseness would do anything to keep you under its spell— to maintain its hold over you.

Once we understand that he, who would "persecute" whatever right-use-ness we have finally found about our person, has to be inferior to it. Which is why he is doing it. Once we understand that, and are wise to it, then we should rejoice and be glad. Our reaction should be, "Well, I certainly must be making great progress." This should be our attitude about anything or anyone who would downgrade our right-use-ness of life once we have attained it. Because certainly we are among those described in this last beatitude by the words, "Blessed are they."

This still leaves a need for something to be said about martyrdom. No one would ever demean the martyrs of all ages for their courage, their heroism and their final sacrifice of the body itself for a cause they deemed greater than themselves.

To many this represents the supreme attainment. And well they might for those who were persecuted for their faith in these long ago biblical times. They probably looked for their strength in the seeming martyrdom of their Wayshower, Jesus Christ—SEEMING martyrdom, that is, according to their limited unfoldment at that time.

While all such souls stand tall in our esteem, we are called upon to learn something here and borrow from their experience—something greater. To begin with, Jesus was not forced into such martyrdom. What He went through, He did by choice. Read the Bible carefully, and you will note that the officials in that episode, that is the important ones—all tried to get him NOT to go through the crucifixion.

But Jesus had a purpose here—that of taking death upon His own person—then overcoming it. To prove, in effect, to His followers, "Because I live, ye shall live also," overcoming the last enemy, death itself, for man. Thus, He could and did say, "Be of good cheer, I have overcome the world."

Thus, too, He was able to continue to prove His reason for coming, which was, "I am come that they might have life, and that they might have it more abundantly." Yes, the whole theme of His teaching was the unfoldment of a spiritual consciousness, so positive, that finally nothing in the outer could ever intimidate one who possessed that consciousness.

Therefore, let our attention here no longer stop at martyrdom, lest we draw the same to ourselves. Rather, let our attention here, as we leave The Beatitudes, be centered anew on the attainment of such a consciousness of life—that brooks no intimidation from without and makes us look even higher than martyrdom!

Spiritual Meditation

The Ten Commandments that Moses received on Mount Sinai are the heart of Judaism. The

Sermon on The Mount is the heart of Christianity. But they are one and the same Law. Moses stated the Law. Jesus explained the highest way to obey it. The "Thou shalt not" of The Ten Commandments is replaced by words "Blessed are ye" in The Sermon on The Mount. Each statement of the Sermon says that we shall be blessed when we attain certain attitudes of mind. The Decalogue's stern delineation of right and wrong is mitigated in The Beatitudes to a compassionate appeal for righteous thinking and feeling.

The Beatitudes state the Law (Lord or Higher Law of our good) with love. Each of its statements pointedly makes clear to our understanding that there is a CONDITION to be passed before the fruits or results can be enjoyed. In other words, in each instance there has to be a certain ATTITUDE on our part before we can have its state of being with its results. The Sermon on The Mount or The Beatitudes in no sense of the word is intended to abrogate the revered Ten Commandments or The Decalogue. But rather to teach us how to fulfill the same Laws of God in a higher spiritual manner. Learning to love the Higher Laws of our good is the final answer; not just obeying them because we should!

"Delight thyself in the Lord (Higher Laws of God), and he shall give thee the desires of thine heart."

Psalms 37:4

NEW TESTAMENT

PART V.

"PALM SUNDAY,
PRELUDE TO MIRACLES"

"And when they drew nigh unto Jerusalem,
and were come to Bethpage, unto the Mount of
Olives, then sent Jesus two disciples, Saying
unto them, Go into the village over against
you, and straightway ye shall find an ass tied,
and a colt with her: Loose them, and bring
them to Me."

"All this was done, that it might be fulfilled
which was spoken by the prophet, saying, Tell
ye the daughter of Sion, Behold, thy King cometh unto thee, meek, and sitting upon an ass,
and a colt the foal of an ass."

"And a very great multitude spread their garments in the way; others cut down branches
from the trees, and strawed them in the way.
And the multitudes that went before, and that
followed, cried, saying, Hosanna to the son of
David: Blessed is He that cometh in the Name
of the Lord; Hosanna in the highest."

"And when He was come into Jerusalem, all
the city was moved, saying, Who is this? And

the multitude said, This is Jesus the prophet of Nazareth of Galilee. And Jesus went into the temple of God, and cast out all them that sold and bought in the temple, and overthrew the tables of the moneychangers, and the seats of them that sold doves. And said unto them, It is written, My house shall be called the house of prayer; but ye have made it a den of thieves. And the blind and the lame came to him in the temple; and he healed them."

Matthew 21: 1 thru 14

Let us enter into what I consider one of the five greatest occasions of the calendar year. Palm Sunday, properly utilized, is a kind of prelude to miracles. On this particular occasion we should behold no slackening on our part. Rather a doubling of our attention Godward. Doing the things that are important. Opening ourselves totally to Him.

Now, you know, that we have been giving ourselves to highlights of the Old Testament and highlights of the New. That we have really been learning the meaning of the Bible. So that from now on we can read in a very practical light—

every section, every part. Because it has been made to have a real down-to-earth meaning for us personally.

What we are considering this time is an historical event. We have already learned that the Bible consists of parables, allegories, and finally historical events. Even as parables and allegories must be read for their meaning to self, even so must every historical event be read for the same reason. The parable, the allegory and the historical event are merely the "racks" upon which the "spiritual meat" is hung. And you must digest that meat for your own person, when you read any section of the Bible. Why? Because the Bible is the story of you—the gradual involvement of the Spirit of God in man, and the gradual evolvement of that Spirit into form.

This historical event, Palm Sunday, has great spiritual meat for us. To decipher it, we must turn to its polar words that relate the meaning to ourselves, and to its polar keys in the forms of phrases that do the same.

The first polar word is found in the opening description of the event. "And when they drew nigh unto Jerusalem, and were come to Beth-page, unto the Mount of Olives, then Jesus sent two disciples." The key polar word here for deep Truth students is the word "Jerusalem." Jerusalem had a very special connotation to all the people of those days in the known world. It was the city known as the spiritual mecca of its time, where the most learned people and the most spiritually unfolded souls resided or visited.

To give you something of its importance, it has been said of the United States that the four most different cities are Boston, New York, New Orleans and San Francisco. They symbolize the fact that the word "city" represents the kind of people that make it up. Boston is as different from New York as day and night. The same with New Orleans. The same with San Francisco.

Now we come back to the word "Jerusalem." Again I emphasize that it was known as the city, which had the greatest spiritual unfoldment of its day—the most learned people. Jesus was at the peak of His fame on this occasion. What He did on this day was purposely done in this great city. Why? That the most learned, spiritually, might witness what He came to represent.

You, who are receptive. You, who are now open. You, who are able to probe the depths of Truth, intellectually at least. You, who are able to go directly to your God. YOU ARE THE JERUSALEM OF TODAY! Thus, you should be able to get the most out of this historical occasion. Because of this unfoldment, you are going to have one of the deepest, most moving experiences of your life.

Note here that Jesus, having come to Jerusalem, ". . . sent two disciples, saying unto them, Go into the village over against you and straightway you will find an ass tied, and a colt thereof with her: loose them and bring them to Me. And if any man say ought unto thee, ye shall say, The Lord hath need of them, and straightway he will send them. All this was done that it might be fulfilled which was spoken by the prophet saying. . . ." From there on, it goes into a description of what the prophet said.

What I want to bring to your attention here is that Jesus was well versed in Hebrew scriptures. He knew all the prophecies. He knew that which He symbolized and represented. And to convey the depth of what He had to bring to the people, He complied with what had been written according to prophecy. All of which was that this person would come unto Jerusalem "riding on an ass and a colt the foal of an ass." He asked that the same circumstances be His. So that the people would know that the prophecy was being fulfilled.

There is nothing wrong about that. I have merely explained why Jesus did it. If He could not perform what He came unto us to represent, then it would prove sheer folly. But He knew that He came in the Name of the Lord, and would prove so. The term "Lord" is practically on every page of your Bible—dating back thousands of years before Jesus. It means God, of course. But it also means God as Law, the Higher Law. That Higher Law is God's plan for you and for me. Jesus came to personalize it. To show what the Law could do for any person, and through him—for others. Finally, He was called the Lord for that same reason.

Next, we go to the prophecy itself, and this is indeed interesting. But before we do, note that, "All this was done that it might be fulfilled, which was spoken by the prophet, saying, (and here is the prophecy) Tell ye the daughter of Sion." "Sion" is the key polar word here, and its meaning is that it is the name for the most unfolded spiritual people of that day. Yes, the Sionist owned the greatest response Godward at that time. Therefore, such were the ones most responsive to a great Truth needed to be known. Note, too, that the prophecy refers to the "daughter of Sion." "Daughter" symbolizes the feeling nature of man. And that is as it should be, because in the beginning God created us so as to be able to work directly upon our subconscious or feeling nature. Then up to the canvas of our conscious mind, and out into the world.

Again I would emphasize this: You are the "Sion" of today. The same as you are the "Jerusalem" of today. You know that you must develop the same beliefs in your subconscious that let Jesus operate from heaven within. You do not get into heaven by another person save to the degree that He shows you what you must have to receive it. Then you develop the consciousness. Having long since learned to think of yourself in this fashion—as one who has the consciousness—you put yourself into this category, "For he that hath, to him shall be given:

. . ." (Mark 4:25) You know that the only way upward is to get it into consciousness. So you are the "Sion" of today, even as you are the "Jerusalem" of today!

Remember, here, that Jesus is bringing into practicality all of the illumination and wisdom of those great prophets who went before Him. An Abraham, who was open to a covenant from God for a new land. A Jacob, who revealed you have never found yourself until you have "wrestled with a Man," the Divine Self, that Jesus knew—and become that Man. A Moses, who was nothing until he found the I AM, which again is that Man, the Divine Self. From such he was told that he could be a leader, that he could do mighty things for his people. And he did!

Jesus makes no claim of Himself for any healing, any prosperity, any order, any harmony released through His person. He made that most clear in John 14:10. You cannot twist the words, ". . . The Father that dwelleth in me . . ."— this individualization, this Divine Self—"He doeth the works." Neither Abraham, Jacob, Joseph, Moses or Jesus performed anything

miraculous until they came to know they represented a Being greater than themselves, even
God's individualized Presence within them.
Each challenge afforded them the opportunity to partake of His Presence mighty in the
midst of them. Release His action. Work out the
problem. Be left on higher ground. With a little
more of God come forth through them.

Jesus was bringing all of this. Recognizing all
those who went before, and adding to their
knowledge in this journey into light.

And this prophecy was, "Tell ye the daughter
of Sion, Behold thy king cometh unto thee,
meek and sitting upon an ass and a colt, the foal
of an ass." So Jesus got the ass and the colt and
rode into the city of Jerusalem, as the prophecy
cited. He did it because He knew that He represented all unfoldment that had gone before, and
now truly was—the very Nature of the Lord
God. He came in the Name of the Lord, the
Nature of the Higher Law of God. He came as
its Word. And that word comes to us—idea by
idea to handle any challenge in this outer world.

I set up an experiment opening Lent each
year, taking three ideas from the Word of God

—opposites of three possible negative conditions through which people were going. Our Truth background made us to know that these three negative conditions were there, because up until then—this was our personal word about our world. The word is our definite thought. Everything good or bad in our world is made by our word. Now we were going to make the Word of God—our Word through Lent. No longer having these sides of our life supported by our negative word. So we looked to the counter opposites of our old negative word—the wholeness instead of sickness, the supply instead of lack, the harmony instead of disorder. We opened ourselves totally to these three ideas of the Word of God to be completed by Easter. Thus, we allowed that Word to move into our consciousness in three sides of our lives.

On Palm Sunday I would ask how many had their three goals worked out as yet. I dared to hope that perhaps many of them now had two completed. In which they allowed the Word of God, backed by the whole of His Spirit, to come into their consciousness and write its Higher Law "in their inward parts." So that three new conditions were being supported, as against the old ones no longer upheld, because they had mentally turned their backs on the old conditions. For they had sacrificed that kind of thinking. For they had been giving themselves to the Word of God. And the very Spirit of God, that backs it up, had brought that Word into flesh in two sides of their lives to some degree already. This was my prayer.

So they were healing in the spots where they needed wholeness. They were prospering in the places where they needed supply. And they were harmonizing in the corners where they needed order. They intended that all three sides of their lives needing help—by means of the Word becoming flesh—would be resurrected by Easter. This would show that they were not among religious people—just wandering in awe. Who merely looked at the Palm Sunday episode every year, watched Jesus ride into Jerusalem, and felt themselves to have no part—save homage. They were equipped to know that they had to get into the picture. That they must receive the Word, become the Word —and let it take over their lives. That someone else could only show them the way to do it. That this is the realistic kind of homage they could pay to all the wayshowers who went before them, culminating in Jesus Christ.

Come to realize, then, that God wants to work through your consciousness with His Word as much as anyone who has ever lived— an Abraham, a Jacob, a Joseph, a Moses, a Jesus—all of the great demonstrators. They were simply wayshowers to the use of the Word. So let this Word become your definite thought about three specific sides of your life, too. You know you do not do the work of Spirit behind the Word. You just have to become the definite thought of what God wants done, which is the Word—in both your knowing and feeling. Then, the whole of God's Spirit performs through that Word, and turns it into flesh.

It is not just mental manipulation on your part, in which by psychology you change your world. You are changing your world here by nothing less than that which was used by the great wayshowers. You are doing the same thing. As the Bible puts it in Zachariah 4:6, "Not by might, nor by power. . . ." (in the outer) ". . . but by my Spirit, saith the Lord" (these things are done). You are just seeking to get out of the way by mentally turning your back on your old way of thinking. Then mentally becoming in thought what God is doing in three sides of your life. Thus you have done exactly what the wayshowers before you have done. You are willing. You are ready. You are now going to receive. The Word shall become flesh.

Next, the disciples went and did as Jesus commanded. Got this equipment (the ass and the colt) together. He then rode into the city, as the prophecy had said. Yes, "They brought the ass and the colt and they put on them their clothes and set Him thereon." Such is the way the prophecy said He would enter into the city.

Here, let us get back to what He represents. He comes in the Name of the Lord, the Nature of the Higher Law of God for you. And this Nature works by means of its Word. You are letting that Word become you in three sides of your life. And the Word is enforced by Spirit.

Now, what takes place is what has already been taking place in you. In the historical story it says, "Now a very great multitude spread their garments in the way." They took off their clothes and threw them down before Jesus sitting on an ass, with a colt alongside Him. Coming down the path, they strawed their garments in the way. This must be likened to you. You have strawed your old garments, the three old conditions upon which you have mentally turned your back. You have thrown them down in front of the Word of God—once and for all.

Think of Jesus now in depth. He personalized the Word of God. This Word has every capacity to write its own Higher Laws "in your inward parts" personally, too. The Higher Law of wholeness for your eyes, or heart, or back. The Higher Law of supply sufficient and to spare for that side of your life. The Higher Law of order, harmony and happiness for your human relations.

So you are throwing down your sickness once and for all before this Word. You are throwing down your financial limitation before this Word. You are throwing down your disorder before this Word. And there is no arrangement for you to pick them up again. Therefore, the Word of God is moving into you—its definite idea for each side of your life needing help. And Holy Spirit behind that Word is overwhelming your consciousness. This is happening to you!

"The multitudes that strawed their garments . . ." reducing this to you, means all the multitude of thoughts that supported the three old conditions. All those old ways of thinking. The multitude of them—you have laid them down before the Word. You have sacrificed them once and for all.

That is a great thing to get rid of—all these old, negative thoughts. It is amazing how some people, who are not unfolded enough as yet, hold on to hard facts in their lives. They grab hold of them, lay hold of them, stretch them, "milk" them, tell everyone over and over again how hard things are to overcome.

It is like the bear in the old story, you know, that came into a camp where they had a pot of goodies boiling. No one was looking, so the bear grabbed the pot. Rushed off into the woods, and the more he squeezed the pot, the more it burned him. This is the way people are with their hard conditions. They never let go of them. Rather squeeze them all the more to themselves.

For example, I could say to you, "Put them

down on the floor. We have an arrangement with the custodian to cart them away afterward." Then perhaps you would say, "Well, maybe I will do that." So you put them down, and then furtively pick them up again. Oh, no! Lay them down, and let them lie there. Get rid of them. Stop letting them belabor your mind.

Let your mind be totally open to what Jesus represents here. As the Word—He is coming into Jerusalem. He is coming into Sion. You are the Jerusalem of today. You are the Sion of today. Jesus represents the Word of God, which would write its Higher Law "in your inward parts." How? By the Nature of God, His Spirit, not by anything less. Remember, ". . . By my Spirit, saith the Lord," (these things are done) —but you must be willing to become mentally what it wants to do in you. You must believe that this Word, now becoming definitely yours about three sides of your life and backed by the whole of God's Spirit, can easily work this out.

There is nothing big, nothing little to the Spirit of God—there is just an answer. And you are letting it possess you by means of its Word—instead of the hard facts of the old conditions.

You have put these garments down. Down in front of the Word, that is coming into your consciousness and writing its Higher Law "in your inward parts." You have thrown your old, negative garments down, and you are going to leave them there.

"And others cut down branches from the trees and strawed them in the way." And there, from this historic act comes the title, "Palm Sunday." The overwhelming majority of trees were palm trees. So when they cut the branches, they almost had to be palm branches. But the branches will not do anything for you unless you understand that in the place of the old garments you threw down, you are now offering up to the Word of God—the meaning of palm branches —which is praise, and which, spiritually interpreted, means spiritually beholding.

If you are really praising God on Palm Sunday, you are spiritually beholding what His Word is doing in you in the place of the old conditions you put down. Yes, you are seeing now in your mind's eye only what God is doing there. This is your definite thought.

The highest form of praise is spiritually beholding that which is unseen of the world. This is the quickest way to release the fulfillment of your need, which is already prepared for you in God.

"And the multitudes that went before, and that followed . . ." in the story—are the people that went before and that followed Jesus. But, in you, they are all those multitudes of thought that went before the Word, and that follow. They are now crying, not an incantation of sorrow and misery, but of great joy, "Hosanna to the son of David." In the story, this indicated that the lineage of Jesus was David. But they go on to cry, "Blessed is He that cometh in the Name of the Lord." This is the Word. And it is coming into you now, in the Name of the Lord, the Nature of God—according to His Higher Law or Plan. It is working itself directly into your subconscious.

Yes, "Blessed is He that cometh in the Name of the Lord" (Higher Law of God for those parts of your life needing help, and becoming flesh there).

THE BIBLE AS THE STORY OF YOU

The passage concludes by saying, "And when He was come into Jerusalem, all the city was moved." Take it out of the historical account. You are the Jerusalem of today. Why? You are now much unfolded. And when the Word of the Lord, to perform its work, comes into you as it is doing now—"all the city was moved." Are you moved? Are you lifted? Are you airborne? Do you feel this Word taking over and writing its Higher Law "in your inward parts?" I have the sense that your whole consciousness has been moved.

In the story, the city of Jerusalem was moved, saying, "Who is this?" A natural response, of course. They wanted to know who He was. "And the multitude said, This is Jesus the prophet of Nazareth of Galilee." In other words, this is the prophet from this little town out here. But you and I know what He represents. This is the Word of God taking over completely in three sides of our subconscious and proving that we, too, can have a resurrection by Easter. That Word now completely dominates. Becomes our definite thought of what is going to happen!

And then we are told in the story, "And Jesus went into the temple." The temple of what? Some brick and mortar way back in Jerusalem in that day? Yes, in the story. But the temple we are talking about here is your temple. "Know ye not that ye are the temple of God, and that the Spirit of God dwelleth in you?" (I Corinthians 3:16)

And Jesus, symbolizing to us what He really was—the Word—is now coming into your temple. And what is that Word doing? "He cast out all them that sold and bought." In the historical story, those operating the temple were using it as a merchandising mart.

In you, what is the Word casting out today? It is casting out all those multitudes of thoughts that produced the three negative things in your life. By letting them absorb all your attention, you were letting them buy and sell your divine heritage for a "mess of pottage." Now all of that is cast out.

"And overthrew the tables of the money-changers." In the story, that merely meant people came from distant places, and brought their form of bartering to the temple. Only to be shortchanged, rather than receive a fair exchange for their means of bartering.

What does this mean to you today? The Word is doing precisely this same thing in you now. It is casting out, turning over anything in you that has been shortchanging you. Those old thoughts, those old feelings in which you have persisted. The Word of God, because you are letting it, is overturning them, turning those thoughts over, overturning anything in you that has been shortchanging you. Those old thoughts, those old feelings—converting them to God's full value—thoughts that are now aligned with Him.

"And overthrew the seats of them that sold doves." What does that mean to you today? The "dove" symbolizes peace of mind. Where is there anything in this outer world, that has found seating in you today and destroyed your peace of mind? What from television? What from the newspapers? What from the people about you—at work—at play? The Word, if you really want it to happen and let it in—will cast out that which has disturbed you up 'til now, and give you peace of mind.

"And Jesus said unto them, It is written, My house shall be called the house of prayer, but ye have made it a den of thieves." Even so the Word of God, that Jesus represented, has said this to you. What should it mean to you today? That your house of consciousness has returned to being a house of prayer. That it is open only to the Word of God. That it is all that is going to govern your life, working out three things in your life to prove its efficacy. Now you understand that, and that your house of spiritual consciousness is back to being a house of prayer. There is nothing in you that longer represents a den of thieves. Nothing in you that robs you of your divine heritage. You are back with God!

"And the blind and the lame came to Him in the temple; and He healed them." What should this mean to you today? Let whatever is blind and lame in you come to the Word of God now governing your consciousness, and be healed. Yes, whatever is blind in you—if it is physical, even that. But more than that, whatever yet is in you that does not know the way in which your three goals are going to work out. Let that blindness of yours be healed by the Word. You now will know the thing to do. It will come to you. This will work out. No one can stop it except you. Give your blindness totally to God.

And whatever is lame in you—if it is physical, even that. But more than that, whatever yet is in you that has handicapped the working out of your three goals—some belief of yours. Let that lameness of yours be healed by the Word. This is the great work. One of the best times to be with the Word is when you are given a background, such as on Palm Sunday. The Word now compounds itself. You are nearer to releasing it than you ever have been. And all three goals of yours are going to be reached. Because Palm Sunday for you—HAS BEEN A PRELUDE TO MIRACLES!

Spiritual Meditation

"Blessed is He that cometh in the Name (Nature) of the Lord (Law)." This means that Jesus came in the Nature of the Higher Law or God's Plan for our lives, and made that Nature plain to us because He was the "Word made flesh."

This Word of God comes to us today idea by idea even as it came to Jesus. Thus on Palm Sunday, even as they of old, we lay down the garments of three old ideas of limitation once and for all (those ideas we decided to cast off or sacrifice at the outset of Lent). And we place palm branches of praise before three Christ ideas of the Word as a symbol of final and utter acceptance (of those three ideas from God we decided at the outset of Lent to realize in the place of the old).

Now the Spirit of God, which does its work in keeping with its Law and through its Word, casts out all those beliefs in you that would buy and sell your divine heritage, shortchange you and destroy your peace of mind.

Finally that Spirit, having written its Law by means of its Word into your subconscious, makes its appearance in your world. So that in your flesh, human relations and finances—you shall see God!

". . . And all flesh shall know that I the Lord am thy Saviour and thy Redeemer. . . ."

Isaiah 49:26

NEW TESTAMENT

PART VI.

"EASTER SHOULD MEAN, FINDING YOUR ASCENSION"

". . . The words that I speak unto you I speak not of myself: but the Father that dwelleth in me, He doeth the works." John 14:10

". . . I go unto the Father: for my Father is greater than I." John 14:28

". . . It is expedient for you that I go away: for if I go not away, the Comforter will not come unto you: . . ." John 16:7

". . . Christ in you, the hope of glory."
Colossians 1:27

This segment is, "Easter Should Mean, Finding Your Ascension." And that is where the emphasis is going to be. As a kind of preface, may I share these thoughts before I begin the subject proper.

Today, born I suppose mostly from despair, there is a great deal of philosophy coming into bloom emphasizing humanism. And this is good. We could certainly use all the fine human beings we can get. I think we all would agree on that. But I want to cite something deeper here. "Things that are seen do not come of things which appear," the Bible tells us in effect. In other words, real wisdom does not originate from the brain, which is the mistake of human reasoning. Unless we capture the deep Truth that the brain is only an instrument for something greater, we have not found ". . . the Way, the Truth and the Life."

We have had a marvelous time relating self to the whole of the Bible—making it come alive so that we can read it easily and in a practical manner. Certain things have become quite apparent, and have stayed with us.

Abraham, the first literal person in the Bible, by himself was no more than the rest of us. The thing that made him distinctive was that he recognized a covenant from a Being greater than himself, and a new land he was to enter through that covenant.

Jacob was so mentally clever that he easily triumphed over his brother—who was basically just physical. But he never found the answer to his life until, as the Bible put it, he "wrestled with a Man all through the night" in his greatest hour of need. And that "Man" was the individualization of God in him, the Divine Self, that took him to the heights possible to every person.

Moses started out with a great temper and a deep inferiority complex. Yet he became one of the greatest men of all time. But only after the appearance in the flaming bush of the "I AM." From that Presence he was told to say to his people, "I Am hath sent me unto thee." In other words, he too laid hold of something greater than self, a Being larger than he. Knowing himself to be its manifesting nature, by it this man was elevated to one of the greatest leaders the world has ever known.

Elijah, another of the greatest prophets, also had no answers until he represented a Being greater than himself. Then he was able to overcome the current idols of man of that day. All of which stands as an example for all time in the overcoming of enslavement to the outer.

Elisha followed, and continued to pyramid this great work we have seen happen through humans, who contacted that which was greater than their outer selves. It is usually overlooked; but Elisha, apart from other miracles, even raised a young man from death to life. Not by his human self, but through representing a Being greater than he, yet individualized right with him.

In all that I have told you, we have before us a journey into light—a growing understanding of what we are, who we are, and where we are going. It is pyramided gradually up to and including Jesus Christ, through whom it was brought to a crescendo.

All of us benefit from the great ones who leave hallmarks. What culminated in Jesus was a culmination of what THAT SOMETHING can do in the lives of each one of us. The greatness of these men was not that which pointed to themselves, but that which revealed the heritage of each one of us.

Since this that they found—culminated itself in a Jesus, the greatest outcropping of this power—I thought that I would share with you in detail here what this is all about. Boiled down, it amounts to the inside story of you!

Throughout all of His teachings Jesus tried to show those who listened to him—how he was related to the Father. And to teach them that they were related to the Father in exactly the same way. Over and over again He tried in different ways to explain what? That God lived within them. That God was everywhere, of course, but individualized within them. That God had no pleasure in their dying through sickness, poverty, unhappiness and frustration. The Bible's description of this was, "For I have no pleasure in the death of him that dieth, saith the Lord God: wherefore turn yourselves, and live ye." (Ezekiel 18:32)

So turn to that Source, God's presence and power within you. Turn away from the outer. Turn to that Source as these great souls I have enumerated did—AND LIVE. In other words, hook your branch back to the tree—that the sap may flow. That sap is the substance, which is not of this world. I coined the phrase that it is a "know how of God" for any side of your life from the realm of His divine ideas.

Yes, there is a life substance or "know how of God" that belongs to you for your body. There is a love substance or "know how of God" that belongs to you for your human relations. There is a prosperity substance or "know how of God" that belongs to you for your financial affairs. You would not think very much of a spider, that refused to spin its web from something within, which is its substance—instinctively. But man has free will. He can just go on trying to make it by himself—or finally learn there is a substance or know how that can enter his consciousness from God for his world.

In Jesus we witnessed this, and that it was a culmination of a practice from Abraham down. We need to latch onto the same secret. Never did Jesus assume to do anything miraculous of Himself. ". . . Not of myself: but the Father that dwelleth in me, He doeth the works," were His words—speaking of the miracles, which people attributed to Him. The same thing that Moses said, pertinent to the "I AM" commanding him.

But it was difficult for people to understand, then, just as it is hard for them to understand, today. So we have not fully laid hold of the ladder of ascension. It should not be something we associate with the end of life. It is for us throughout life. Yes, to ascend over our difficulties, not of self, but by the Father within. Jesus' remedy for life's ills—as with those great souls who went before Him—was that of spiritual resurrection rather than human resignation to one's fate. That any fate can be lifted by the same means these wonderful souls had. That this means was the Father, the Being that is everywhere equally present, but individualized in each one of us as the Christ.

The Christ comes from the Greek word, Christos. It is the Greek word for the Messiah, that which some great Hebrew prophets prophesized would come. Yes, someone would come, they said, to carry into demonstration the covenant of God individualized in man—the "I Am," this Divine Spark, That Something greater than the outer self of man. The word, Christ, from the Greek word, Christos, comes to us from the Greeks because they happened to make the first translation of the Bible from the Hebraic and Aramaic. But it means this Messiah in us all. Someone would still come to carry on the light in all of its possibiliities, they prophesied—which had been demonstrated to some degree by all of these great souls we have reviewed in advance of Jesus.

Let us understand what that means to us, in describing the within of Jesus—who fully demonstrated the Christ. You have depicted there the potential of yourself. There is no basic difference in content. It is a matter of usage. After all, even Jesus was not called the Christ until He had done a number of things. That which added up to evidence of someone who had totally found that Being greater than His outer self.

Now there were in the person of Jesus two distinct regions. There was the outer man, Jesus. Then there was the central, living, real part of Him which was the very Spirit of God— the Son of God. And that was the Christ. It is no different than what is in you. For remember, Jesus said it is written in the older scriptures, referring to the Old Testament in Psalm 82:6, "Ye are gods; and all of you are Children (Sons) of the Most High."

You can never be God everywhere equally

present, only the individualization of Him, that
is deep within you. God so loved you that He
put Himself—that individualized part of Him—
in you. Not the whole, mind you, but the individualization. For did not Jesus say, "One is
greater than I, even the Father."

So it is then, that each one of us has two
regions of being. One, this fleshly, mortal part,
which of itself can so often just feel its weakness
and inefficiency in all things. But there, at the
central-most part of our being, is that which in
our highest moments makes itself known to us as
more than the conqueror of all things. It is the
Christ, the individualization of God, the
anointed of a power that works beyond time
and space and all human limitations. It is the
very Name or Nature of the Father within you.
It is there, the same as in Jesus. And it is high
time this became—the motivation of our lives!

We must all realize that it was the Christ or
Father within, that made Jesus what He was.
Never once did Jesus assume to do anything as of
Himself—as far as miracles were concerned.
"Not of myself: but the Father that dwelleth in
me, He doeth the works," Jesus said. The Father

within, then, is the Christ, just as the I Am of a
Moses was the Father within. The covenant that
gave a new land to Abraham came also from the
Father within. The "Man" that Jacob, for all his
cleverness, had to wrestle with throughout the
night in order to find his Real Self, was the
Father within, the Principle of God in man.

Our power, therefore, to help ourselves to the
fullest—and others, lies in comprehending this
deepest of all Truths. That the same Christ lives
within us, that lived in Jesus. It is the individualization of Himself, that God has put within
us. That lives there with constant love and
desire to spring to the circumference of our
being as our all sufficiency in our journey
through life.

Our basic weakness, as humans, is that we get
our eyes fixed on the external of our being—
the external region. In this way we lose consciousness of this indwelling, ever-active God,
our Father, at the central-most part of our
being. And so we see ourselves, in keeping with
others like ourselves, who have lost their way.
What happens to them, we let happen to us. We
become convinced in this way of the limitations

of man. We see ourselves sick, weak and in so many ways miserable, because others are. We say, we are of the same species, and so it is our common lot.

But it is not! Jesus did all His mighty works, not because He was given some greater or different power from that which God has given us. Not because he was in some different way a Son of God, and we just Children of God. But because the same Divine Spark, implanted in each one of us—was fanned to a flame in Him.

When Jesus said, "Come unto me and I will give you rest," He could not have meant His own person. How could He? He had to know there would be millions who could not reach him. He was speaking then of the Christ or the Father within. Meaning NOT—come unto me, Jesus, but come unto the Father within, the Christ. Yes, come out of the mortal part of yourself. Where there is sickness and sorrow and frustration so much of the time. Come up out of it! Come up out of it into the Christ part of you where the Father dwells. There you will find rest in living, the kind of rest that comes from divine answers to your problems as you go along.

This kind of spiritual reasoning helps us to understand another of Jesus' statements that has puzzled so many, "No man cometh unto the Father save by me." For anyone in religion to try to cause a division among spiritual seekers through this—is utterly stupid. All that we find in the New Testament, we find because of the Old Testament. We are one people going in one direction—to one God. What does this passage really mean? NOT that the only way you can find the Father is through Jesus. After all, Moses found the Father through the "I Am." Jacob found the Father through the "Man" with whom he wrestled all night long in his tent.

The real meaning of the passage is this. No man can come unto the Father except through the Christ part of himself, or the "I Am" part of himself, or the Father within part of himself. In other words, you cannot find the meaning of your person and the fullness of your being by any outside method. It is from the inside, the deep within. There is no other way!

Another may teach you, show you the way as all of these great wayshowers have. But finally you have to take time in your busy life to learn to retire within. Find time for it—for your own soul. Open yourself to the help that is available there from the Father within. Then there will be ushered into you the substance or know how to meet your every need. Yes, the branch will have been put back on the tree, and sap will flow into it once again. It is a mistake of ours to say, "I am mental first, then I am emotional and finally I am physical." You have "missed the boat"—until you know that you are first spiritual. And have put that FIRST THING first.

The mental, the emotional and the physical should all three rest upon SOMETHING ELSE, with the understanding simply to be its instruments. Then you will have humans, who really reveal something, because they have come into their own. They become the intended Manifesting Nature for a Being greater than themselves. They manifest what God wants done in their lives. This is no "holy Joe" philosophy. This is finding the meaning of life. The "life more abundant"—the health, the order, the jobs, the friends, the ability to do and be what everyone wants.

Jesus was always trying to get the minds of people away from His personality. Trying to fix them on the Father within their own persons as the Source of power for their lives. When toward the last, they were still clinging to His outer self—and that is understandable—He said to them, "It is expedient for you that I go away, for if I do not go away the Comforter will not come unto you." In effect He was saying, "You are spending all your time looking at My personality instead of THAT WHICH My personality is expressing, and which lies within you to do the same."

Again, what He was saying is, that if He remained where they could keep looking at His personality, they would never know that the same Spirit—the indwelling Father, His power —lived within themselves.

Boiled down, the Easter message points out one salient factor. It is this: The greatest homage, the greatest tribute, the finest proof of love we can offer to Jesus, and to the great souls who paved the way for Him—is to follow Him into the ascension.

Where do we begin? Remember your present problem always outlines where you need to go to work—in the sense of garnering the necessary response Godward. What is the Christ again? It is the Name or Nature of the Father within. That which rose up within Jesus, overwhelmed him and produced miraculous results through Him—as He asked in prayer, believing. It will do the same from within you.

Now if you sincerely want the Christ instead of your problem, here are TEN QUICK POINTS I am going to give to you in closing. You can try them out for yourself, and find out if they will revolutionize your life for the better. They surely will help you be open to the One who created you, the Father within you. God over Australia is fine, but not much aid to you unless you know that the same Presence over Australia is individualized right where you are!

Here are the points, as briefly as I can put them:

FIRST, if you want to find the meaning of you, and the full blossom of you, here it is: You must visit the Christ daily. About what? Well, the problem at hand will be good enough for a start. That is why you have it. To make you turn to Him. Now before some of you say, "You are going to give me ten things that I am supposed to be doing. I'm too busy already." Wait a minute! With what are you busy? All day long—at home, in the office, on the street—what enters in—you! Yes, you do an amazing lot of thinking about you. So do not tell me you lack the time. How about some thinking that will revolutionize this outer self you are not too keen about, though you pretend you are. Everybody has time for that which will make self airborne. Part of Truth is talking to yourself. Just do not let anyone see you. Visit the Christ daily.

SECOND, make the visit short. It has nothing to do with time. Only how much realization you get. So seek the feeling that you have made contact. That you have released the Christ. Equate the word, "Christ," with the Living Action of God. Yes, that you have released the Living Action of God onto your problem.

THIRD, in each of your visits, whenever they may happen, ask yourself, "Do I expect results in releasing this Action from On High?" That means—does the bottom of your heart answer, "Yes," when you ask, "Do I expect results?"

FOURTH, if not, do not force it. After all, it may have been a long time since you have done any of this visiting. If you honestly cannot get a "yes" answer in your feelings—that you have contacted the Father within and will receive the results of His Action—just return again and again in your visits until finally the bottom of your heart answers, "Yes." You are just as much created to be a channel for God's Action as a Jesus or a Moses. Remember each visit with God through prayer is cumulative; and if, through it, you get the habit of releasing His Living Action upon each problem that arises, you are going to come off at your best. Gently persist in this practice, and soon you must regularly get the expectancy, "Yes, I have released God's Action onto this case—and will get results."

FIFTH, always close your visit by giving thanks in advance for the Action that is going to happen. Just as though it had already happened. Why? Because that is the quickest way to build up the necessary response so that the bottom of your heart will say, "Yes."

SIXTH, above all, in every visit proclaim, "I

want to demonstrate the Christ—not my problem. I want to demonstrate the Christ, the Living Action of God, to handle this problem."

SEVENTH, here are the acid tests to tell whether you are fibbing or not when you proclaim that you really want this Living Action of God. Did you really visit the Christ today? Only you can answer that. And did you seek to act out your expectancy all through the day following that visit?

EIGHTH, remember the only part of the Truth that you own as yet is the part you act out. Not how many books you have at home. Not how many lectures you have attended. Not how many affirmations you have stacked in a drawer somewhere. Just the part you act out!

NINTH, none of this business of saying, "Well, I'm a regular churchgoer, you know. But I feel that I am unworthy. However, I hope something works out here." That is old stuff. Stop it!

TENTH, recapitulate. It is fun: "Christ in

you, the hope of glory." If you want this Christ, invoked and released, you must visit with the Christ—the Living Action of God. You do not have to strike any holy pose. Just wherever you are, turn to it, if you want the answer to your current problem. And remember, short visits with the Christ are best. But return again and again in those visits until the bottom of your heart answers the question, "Do I expect results?" With this reply, "Yes, I fully expect the Christ, the Living Action of God, to have been released onto this case." Then you shall be able to see the glory or result in your life—as Jesus and these other wonderful souls did. And the glory of the Lord will be the perfect working out of your present problem. This way you will know for sure, that another step upward has been taken by you into your ascension!

Spiritual Meditation

Jesus did all His mighty works, not because He was given some greater or different power from that which God has given us. Not because he was in some different way the Son of God, and we only Children of God. But because the same Divine Spark, implanted in each of us, was fanned into a flame in Him. How? Through keeping His eyes away from the external and centering His thoughts on the central-most part of His being, which is the Christ, the Principle of God in man as well as the Living Action.

When Jesus said, "Come unto Me, and I will give you rest," He was speaking from the Christ or Father within, meaning not, "Come unto Jesus," but rather, "Come unto the Christ." That is, "Come up out of the mortal part of you into the Christ part of you where the Father dwells, and the Father within you will give you rest." The kind of rest that comes from divine answers to your problems.

So, if you want the Christ, the Living Action of God invoked and released in your present problem, you must visit the Christ daily, short visits, and return again and again in those visits until the very bottom of your heart answers, "Yes," to the question, "Do I expect results?" Then shall you see the glory or result in your life. And that glory will be the perfect working out of your problem.

". . . Be of good cheer: I have overcome the world."   John 16:33

NEW TESTAMENT
PART VII.
"REVELATION'S REWARDS"

"He that overcometh shall inherit all things
..." Revelation 21:7

". . . To him that overcometh, will I give to
eat of the tree of life, which is in the midst of
the paradise of God." Revelation 2:7

". . . He that overcometh shall not be hurt of
the second death." Revelation 2:11

". . . To him that overcometh will I give to
eat of the hidden manna, and will give him a
white stone, and in the stone a new name
written, which no man knoweth saving he that
receiveth it." Revelation 2:17

Anyone, no matter what he would accomplish, who thinks he has to crowd it into his
years on this plane BECAUSE THAT IS ALL
THERE IS—to me, that person's consciousness
falls far short of its ability to receive.

Every person should know something of his past. Also, how to make the most out of his present. And something about where he is going in his future.

They have a saying, "You can't take it with you." That is human reasoning again. The surest thing I know is that whatever you have compiled in the way of Truth unfoldment will go with you. That it will play its part in "putting you on velvet" in your ongoing. "Revelation" is the least understood section of the Bible. To most people, it would be a revelation to understand that—Revelation of the Bible means a portrayal of the hidden future of you. Every person is overcoming that in which he finds himself—limitations. And every Truth student wonders what it would be like to have overcome all of the intimidations of the outer world to his person. All of this is wrapped up in Revelation.

Whatever is revealed in this segment of the Bible, I think you will recognize some of the things that have already happened to you. And that, in turn, should make you think of other descriptions in this section, which are also going to be part of your life in your ongoing as a Truth student. So this subject has great meaning, and I have called it, "Revelation's Rewards."

We are first going to consider, "He that overcometh shall inherit all things." This is the direct promise of God to you from Revelation, chapter 21: verse 7. Who does that, whereby he inherits all things? The overcomer! Now everybody at this juncture in his adventure into life wants something—health, peace of mind, prosperity, order, justice—and one of these may be your need of the moment. So the Bible has much to say about the overcomer. He will eventually inherit all of these. For again, Revelation is the Bible's insight into man's hidden future.

In Revelation, chapter 2: verse 7, we are told, "To him that overcometh will I give to eat of the tree of life, which is in the midst of the paradise of God." If you will remember my review of Adam and Eve, which is a parable pertinent to every day of your life, you will recall that the "tree of life" is mentioned—as our goal. Also, that our challenge of and our reason for being kicked out of the Garden of Eden—was eating of the "tree of good and evil" rather than the "tree of life."

Listen again to this promise, "To him that overcometh, to him will I give to eat of the tree of life, which is in the midst of the paradise of God." The "tree of life" means joy, interest, knowledge of God and dominion. So that nothing can frighten or upset you again. When you get that kind of consciousness from eating of the "tree of life," you are in paradise. And paradise is everywhere awaiting you. You do not have to die to get into it. You find it when you have the consciousness for it. That is how you get into it. And there is no other way. This is not something another can buy for you. You have to earn it yourself in consciousness—which is what you become aware of to the point of conviction.

In Revelation, chapter 2: verse 11, we are told, "He that overcometh shall not be hurt by the second death." As I said earlier, this is the part of the Bible least understood by biblical students. Read it again, "He that overcometh shall not be hurt by the second death." I know that you understand that, but I am going to explain it anyway.

The meaning here is that you die mentally first, before you die physically. And that goes for any sector of your life. In other words, to be detailed about it: If you do not die mentally to your health, you do not experience the second death—sickness. If you do not die mentally to your prosperity and success, you do not experience the second death—lack and failure. If you do not die mentally to harmony and order in your life, you do not experience the second death—inharmony and chaos. Boiled down, the technique, which has been given you in the study of Truth, and which is required here to avoid that second death is, "Keep the cover of your kettle of consciousness on" as far as the outside world is concerned. Such as television, radio, newspapers, and people who do not know how to live and thus are the victims of everything that comes along.

I recently heard a friend describing her reaction to the outside world of our time. She felt led to call the TV station and say, "I want the news, but can't you soften it a little?" But they have to make it sensational. It is their business. So, "Keep the cover of the kettle of your consciousness on—as far as the outside world is concerned. And off—as far as the spiritual world from within is concerned. That the things of God only may be brewed in it." This quote is from Dr. Ervin Seale, Minister Emeritus of the Church of The Truth.

Now that is pretty plain. It does not mean to put your head in the sand. You want to know what is going on in the world—an accurate appraisal of it. But you want to know it for the purpose of sending out help. Not just lying there like a sponge, lapping it up. Or like a newsboy in Miami, some years ago, who used to cry in a very loud voice in order to sell his papers, "The whole world is going to hell." That always got a customer, of course, when nothing else seemed to attract.

Again in Revelation, chapter 2: verse 17, we are told, "To him that overcometh will I give to eat of the hidden manna." You know, it is rather amusing, but "overcoming" has such a forbidden tone to it for most people. Let us look at the "other side of the coin." It will prove fascinating indeed. For it is the route you are traveling as a student of Truth. And everything that I am writing about is a description of you.

"Hidden manna" means heavenly food. So

the Bible asks the question—when you are faced with chaotic situations on television, radio or newspaper or in your own life—do you have spiritual meat to eat to counteract it? Yes, hidden manna is heavenly food, and remember the remarkable thing about manna is that it will not keep. You must use it up today. When you skip a day, you have missed your manna. This, as it is told in the Bible, refers to the inspiration of God.

In other words, you cannot live on yesterday's inspiration. You must have it anew each day of your life. The hidden manna, inspiration direct from God to you—you never lose. It will never grow stale. Just the outer—what it wants you to do for each day, enjoy for each day—to make that day full. Yes, just the outer bit of manna—that is given to you for that day to do—must be used up or *grow stale*. The rest of it, the infinite, unused hidden manna, will never grow stale. You will never lose it. It belongs to you. But it is of no value until you eat of it each day.

Revelation, in the same quotation, goes on to say, "And (I will give to that OVERCOMER who eats daily of the hidden manna) I will give him a white stone." The "white stone" means a sense of the presence of God. It is a sense of having your consciousness made clean, white and pure—in spite of what is going on out here—by which to receive your own. The white stone is a sense of the presence of God for each day.

"Brick," as used in the Bible, symbolizes baseness. But I do not want anyone reading this to get the impression that I disapprove of brick houses or anything like that. I am just pointing out, by contrast, that the white stone, which you are to own for each day of your life, is like marble. It symbolizes nobility from within, holiness or a wholesome outlook totally from within—perfection from within. White symbolizes the spiritual.

Years ago, when people, who were inclined to be psychic, would see an aura around someone—they were almost afraid to mention it. Why? Because others would think they were a little bit odd. Today all such fear is gone. Scientists have now proven scientifically by machinery, that every person has an aura—in color. That it varies in keeping with his consciousness.

They took a woman. Who was known for great love—above all other people in her neighborhood. One who abounded in love. They let her express herself, and the aura came out—orange-red. They took a mathematician, not off the platform, but on. Really gifted in his field. Let him lose himself in that science, and it came out—purple. They took a man of the cloth. Filled with the Holy Spirit. Let him express himself fully, lost in his belief, and it came out—white. So we do not have to concern ourselves about "auras from consciousness" any more. That makes the white stone become more practical to you as you overcome.

Continuing the same quote, Revelation goes on to say, ". . . And in that stone, a new name written, which no man knoweth saving he that receiveth it." The "new name" here means a new nature, a spiritual nature. This belongs to the overcomer. As though born again each day. We all want this, a new nature, a spiritual nature for each day. "And no man knoweth that name," we are told, "Saving he that receiveth it." If you would be an overcomer each day—you receive it. It means simply that in receiving this renewed spiritual nature for each day,

other people will notice the change in conduct
in you. They will notice the change in appearance in you. They will notice the change in
disposition in you. But nobody will know what
has taken place, save you. That it has happened
—because of your overcoming anew each day
through God.

For illustration, the wife may say, "Every
day I pinch myself, he has improved so much."
Never mind what the husband may say about
the wife. The secret here is a new name between
you and God—that happens in this growing,
overcoming you each day. And, is not that
worth knowing? Why should the newspapers,
television and radio stomp us to death, when
this can be our destiny—in spite of what is going
on in the outer world.

Then, in Revelation, chapter 2: verse 26, we
are told, "He that overcometh, and keepeth my
works unto the end, to him will I give charge
over the nations." Interesting? What does it
mean? "Nations" here means all of your faculties. Charge over your faculties. Charge over
your powers, so that you can use them each day.
It does not mean the United Nations. That you

will become a member of this august body. There is not much the United Nations can do—save deliberation and censure. Perhaps that will change for the better in time. Let that be our prayer.

Then from Revelation, chapter 3: verse 5, "He that overcometh, the same shall be clothed in white raiment." "White raiment" means to be clothed in peace, in harmony, in joy—from within. Yes, ". . . That my joy might remain in you, and that your joy might be full." (John 15:11) Revelation 3:5 goes on to say, "I will not blot out his name (this overcomer in each day) from the book of life, but I will confess his name before my Father, and before His angels." Yes, confess this new nature about him, "before my Father and His angels"—Jesus speaking here, of course. All of which is a way of saying poetically, that you may be sure of this as you overcome—all intimidations from the outer each day—one intimidation at a time.

Also, from Revelation, chapter 3: verse 12, we read, "Him that overcometh will I make a pillar in the temple of my God, and he shall go no more out." "No more out" means the overcomer need not be "put out to pasture" for more processing, when he has finally overcome all intimidations from the outer world. Every lifetime is being put to pasture for processing, for unfoldment. And the time will come when nothing out here, through our overcoming, will intimidate us. Yes, having overcome the last outer intimidation of man, the process of overcoming has served its purpose—and is no longer needed.

Thus finally from Revelation, chapter 3: verse 21, we read, "To him that overcometh, (to this degree) will I grant to sit with Me in My throne." Notice it says, not on My throne, but "in My throne"—meaning in My dominion. And dominion here does not mean dominating things, but simply releasing that which God wants done each day in your life. The things He wants expressed in every situation. The releasement of that which is DIVINELY NATURAL. That is His dominion and yours!

Now what is overcoming? Do NOT think it is something frightfully difficult! You are the complex one. Life is simple. We make it hard by our own complexities. It does not mean here asceticism—days and nights of prayer. It means cultivating a real faith in prayer—overcoming the belief that prayer in you will not work. That is a MUST for the overcomer. Prayer in you—overcoming all notions that prayer in you will not work.

You know, in the Far East they teach torture as a means of growing spiritually. Recently, for example, I had the dubious privilege of watching on television one of these fanatics run over by a truck. You probably have seen something similar. Some lie on beds of spikes. We have all seen that stunt. They do not say it verbally, but you get the impression, "How good am I. Others can't do it even for a few moments." But all that happens is—that they get "stuck up." I mean that figuratively, of course. Friends told this about such a fanatic in the Far East. "He held up one of his arms for an entire year." Yes, he succeeded in doing it! Of course, that got him much nearer to God, holding his arm up for one year. No, I think not. Rather a useless arm.

My reaction to this type of approach to spiritual unfoldment is simple enough. When broken glass is strewed all over our streets as an everyday occurrence. When hot coals are standard equipment for our pathways. When spikes have replaced bedsprings. Then I will consider such as a part of spiritual unfoldment. Until then, I will consider the only tests of spirituality to be those which are common to us all. Tests that come by route of natural events, such as sickness to be overcome, lack, unhappiness, frustration, loneliness and so forth. These are the real tests for the overcomer.

Overcoming, then, means breaking with the devil. And understanding once and for all who the devil is—not some creature whipped up on the screen by Hollywood, or on television, or radio, or in books, or on the psychic level. But facing honestly the fact that the devil, as far as you are concerned, is just your own in-a-rut, lower self that has, as yet, not been overcome.

So overcoming means breaking with evil, every suggestion of it, every form of it. Overcoming means breaking off faith in matter—or what is the matter with you? Be it a heart condition, the times, age keeping you from a job, or whatever. Overcoming means, no matter what happens to the body, from a cut finger to cancer, that God can heal it, if you pray believing. Overcoming means—no matter your age or the times—believing God can take you to your true place and letting Him do it. That is overcoming!

To one, who prays believing that this can happen, God does not say to that person—"No, because of the times I can't do it." God does not say to that person, "Sorry you are over seventy, so all I can do for you is put you in an old folks' rest home." God never has and never will say that to the person who prays believing!

Overcoming, boiled down, means this. Stop limiting the Holy One in you. That is the main overcoming. Do not condition your prayers, and God will not then be limited in the new conditions He would bring forth through you— into your world—in spite of the outer world. Overcoming is simply giving no power to the outer—the body, some person or persons, or a business situation. Giving no power to it whatsoever. Rather giving all power to God, and then strangely enough—and it has ever been so —all power in heaven and in earth will be given unto you to break that spell!

Spiritual Meditation

Overcoming has such a forbidding tone to it for most people. There is a need to look at the "other side of its coin" to find its fascination.

Revelation, the Bible's insight into man's hidden future, does just that for you. Not only does it reveal the magnificence of the overcomer's future. But also it makes plain that overcoming must not be looked upon as something frightfully difficult! With self alone trying to do it, perhaps; but with God, no! Why? Because God then gives you the "tree of life" from which to eat; where before, you were mired down from eating of the "tree of good and evil."

The "tree of life" means joy, interest, knowledge of God and dominion—so nothing can frighten or upset you. When you get that, you are in Paradise. And Paradise is everywhere. You do not have to die to get into it. You enter by consciousness. There is no other way!

Overcoming means breaking with the devil or your lower, in-a-rut self. Breaking with evil or the limited beliefs of the race. And breaking with matter—or the person, situation or thing that seems to be the barrier to your good.

In other words, overcoming is simply giving no power to the outer. But most important of all, it means stop conditioning the Holy One within you—IN YOUR PRAYERS! Then God will not be limited in the new conditions He would bring forth through you. So let it be!

OLD AND NEW
TESTAMENTS

BOTH OLD AND
NEW TESTAMENTS

(THE WAY TO GET THE MOST OUT OF THEM)

"Hitherto have ye asked nothing in My Name: Ask, and ye shall receive, that your joy may be made full."   John 16:24

"Call unto Me, and I will answer thee, and shew thee great and mighty things, which thou knowest not."   Jeremiah 33:3

"The Lord is nigh unto all them that call upon Him, to all that call upon Him in Truth."
Psalm 145:18

". . . But they that seek the Lord shall not want any good thing."   Psalm 34:10

"He shall call upon me, and I will answer him: I will be with him in trouble: I will deliver him, and honour him. With long life will I satisfy him, and shew him my salvation."
Psalm 91:15, 16

"The meek will He guide in judgment: and the meek will He teach His way."   Psalm 25:9

"And all things, whatever ye shall ask in prayer, *believing*, ye shall receive."
Matthew 21:22

It seems fitting and proper that I should close this work on the Bible with this added segment. We have reviewed up 'til now—highlights from the Old Testament and highlights from the New—so as to get a proper view of the Bible and know it to be a gradual journey into light. Yes, the involvement of God's Spirit in us, and the evolvement of it into form. In this review, we have already considered the allegories, the parables, the historical sections of the Bible, and some of the prophecies of Revelation.

Now, then, because most people in using the Bible turn at random to its promises, I felt that I should give you an exact method for getting the most out of these promises—the exact keys for unwrapping them. Unwrapping their coverings, so to speak, that you may be able to use them in their most practical relation to yourself.

Thus our subject is, "The Promises." Many people would be quite surprised to learn, that as far as the Judaeo-Christian Bible is concerned, there are two Bibles. The ordinary one, whichever version—King James or American Standard or whatever version you particularly like. This is one Bible. Then there is another

Bible—the Hidden Bible. It lies between the lines.

This Bible is discovered through understanding the key or polar words and phrases found within all its passages. These keys are found, then, in the parables, in the allegories, in the historical sections, and in the prophecies. But it must be emphasized here that these key or polar words and phrases are found also in the individual promises of the Bible, which is our subject for consideration at this time.

First, you need to know that these promises in the Bible are statements of Higher Law. Always remember that! Each promise that you find, and they are strung from Genesis to Revelation —each such promise is a statement of Higher Law.

It is this Hidden Bible that heals the body, melts away our difficulties, and teaches us the things that matter. This Hidden Bible gives us real knowledge—not just intellectual doctrine, dogma and creed. Yes, definite knowledge which we can realize, and when we do, our lives will be changed to that degree from that moment henceforth. Just as it is the negative suggestion we accept, which brings harm into our lives; even so, it is the instruction from the Hidden Bible, which we accept through realization, that changes our lives for the better.

The Hidden Bible does just that. It puts the new thing into your subconscious, and there it goes right to work. The outer, surface history of the Bible, WHEN IT IS READ ONLY AS HISTORY, such as the sacking of Jerusalem three different times—does not do anything for you. But the Hidden Bible does. It keeps you from mistakes. It heals you, prospers you and dissolves your fears.

Now this Hidden Bible is packed and crammed with real knowledge. And it is the individual verse or what sometimes seems almost half a verse, that contains the great power of God. Within each is found this power, and it does the work in your life. It goes right into your soul.

The first one we are going to consider is from Jeremiah, the 33rd chapter: 3rd verse, "Call upon Me," God says, "and I will answer thee

. . ." Now this was intended not just for Jeremiah, otherwise why was it written down? It is for everybody. And God said, "Call upon me and I will answer thee. . . ." When it says "call" that is your polar word, your key word. It has special meaning for you. When it says "call," it means you are a little distance away. It means people, who are not having a sense of the Presence of God. It means people, who are in difficulty, because they are away from God.

Some people seem to think that God will not help them unless they are very, very good or deserving. Fortunately that is not true. Here is a good illustration—that of a good mother. When you are a little tot, you think nothing of going to your mother with jam all over your face, dirt on your hands and asking something of her. And, within her ability, she gladly fulfills your request, if it is worthwhile—paying no attention to the jam and the dirty hands.

This is equally in keeping with the nature of God. Consider this statement of His Higher Law, "Call upon me and I will answer thee, and shew thee great and mighty things. . . ." There are no strings on that. Just "call." Not under any other certain conditions. Then what? ". . . And shew thee great and mighty things, which thou knowest not." Not our faults, but wonderful things about ourselves—wonderful working outs.

When you get into the Hidden Bible, it is not an escape. One who finds the Hidden Bible must mean business—business with God. Then it will take us out of unpleasant conditions.

Suppose one is in debt. Has not the remotest idea of what to do about it, so he goes to the movies. Gets absorbed for about an hour and a half or two hours. Forgets all about his debts. What has become of his problem? Well, his debts are all lined up waiting for him on the sidewalk when he emerges from the theater, saying, "Here I am, daddy." He has not done any harm, but he has only temporarily escaped. But the Hidden Bible teaches and brings the new ideas that will heal. That will get us out of our debt.

Let me give you an exact illustration of this, using another kind of problem. A heavy father, and I am not referring to weight here; but heavy in the sense of trouble pertaining to his son, who had disappeared. This father was told about the Hidden Bible. His first reaction was understandable enough. He said he knew all about the Bible. Had a letter from his church to that effect. Yes, he knew the letter of the Bible, but not the Hidden Bible. So, in particular, he was told about the Hidden Bible. He was told that it would turn him to God in a new way, with a fresh mind. And he agreed to try it out.

That evening he was reading the Hidden Bible, and came upon a verse. He got a new sense of peace, and forgave himself. He had already forgiven his son, but not himself. Then the telephone rang. It was his boy's voice. And the son said, "May I come down to see you?" So he got his answer. Beyond the answer, he got a new hold on divine things. A new hold in the sense of new ability to handle his problems. For no human agency had been able to bring his son to him.

In the case of debt, the debt would somehow be paid off immediately or an extension would be given. Yes, ". . . Great and mighty things, which thou knowest not."

Here is another promise, again a statement of the Higher Law of God, Psalm 145: verse 18, "The Lord is nigh . . ." "Nigh" is your polar word. Near what? Near whom? ". . . Nigh unto all that call upon Him." "Call" is your other polar word. Please note! Irrespective of whether you are good or bad, saint or sinner, member of a church or not, ". . . To all that call upon Him in Truth." "In Truth," that is the important key. It is not just a matter of saying, "Lord, Lord." People have been doing that for years with no results.

You see, this is not like old time theology, dealing with dead, pat theories. No, this is religion as a science. And science means demonstrable fact and repeatable phenomenon. It means that once a chemist comes upon a new formula of ingredients, like that for sulphuric acid; then any other chemist, thereafter, can do the same by repeating the formula and producing the same phenomenon. That is science. Old time theology—I do not mean to criticize but to appraise—is incorrect. It cannot demonstrate, and then repeat that phenomenon. It only holds promises after death, which is a safe place to put them.

Now you are asked to try this out. Take your Bible, consider an individual promise, which is a statement of Higher Law, and look for its key or polar words. Latch on to them. Relate them to yourself. "Milk" that statement and its promise for all that it is worth. Remember, it always contains a CONDITION to be passed by you. And once you have passed the condition, it promises an exact FRUIT or result for you.

Do not take my word for this. Try it out. Yes, "The Lord is nigh. . . ." "Nigh" is the first polar word here. "The Lord is nigh . . . to all that call upon Him in Truth." "Truth" is your last polar word. Just calling out to God, without any realization of His Truth, is not much. Some people think, if they just go through the ceremonies of a church, they are "in." Like so many people would not be without a Bible in the house. But they never use it!

Here is a good illustration of such. A man, whose dad was a great one for the Bible, told this about his father. I waited. He said, "My dad always kept the Bible on the top shelf of the kitchen pantry. It was a very heavy Bible, a good, big one. He always got it down every

Saturday night—and pressed his pants for Sunday." I was not shocked. Are you?

When you think of God with new interest, with new belief, through the Hidden Bible— things happen—now! Psalm 34:10 is our next promise. Again, reminding ourselves that it is a statement of Higher Law with a condition in it to be passed and a fruit to be had, let us consider, ". . . But they that seek the Lord shall not want any good thing." Quite clear, is it not? And exact! Certainly you cannot twist it.

"They that seek the Lord"—the Higher Law, the Plan of God for their case, His exact way for the fulfillment to be made manifest—that is what the "Lord" must mean to you in addition to meaning your "Father God." After all, the word "Lord" is found on just about every page of the Bible. Jesus was not called the Lord until he demonstratedd or personified it. "Lord" then is your polar word. So when "they," meaning any and all of us, truly seek the Higher Law, the Plan of God, what He wants done—and see it taking place in the direction of that for which they have asked—that full, perfect working out —then they, ". . . shall not want any good thing." All of which includes that which they are after at the moment.

You see, the person, who understands, really gives himself, continues to seek and renew his interest in God through the Hidden Bible—gets results! NOT THOSE, who just sit back and do nothing, because they think they are already saved!

The promises of God given to us in the Bible are scientific statements. Just as much as those in chemistry or mathematics or electronics. The biggest obstacle to the Bible is that most people respect it, but do not take it seriously. They think it has some bearing on heaven—if, as, and when we get there—but not here. However, the statement is very plain, "They that seek the Lord—right now—shall not want any good thing."

If a scientific book were put out from a reputable house, and it said that with due consideration of certain statements given in this book, you would get inevitable results—that place would be mobbed! But this is what the Bible does, if you understand the Hidden Bible.

The next promise or statement of Higher Law we are going to consider is from Psalms 91: the 15th and 16th verses, "He shall call upon me, and I will answer him: I will be with him in trouble; I will deliver him, and honour him. With long life will I satisfy him, . . ." A tremendous statement, as well as promise!

What is meant by "long life" here? If we study that for a moment, we will get something worthwhile. What is life? Well, life is not just any experience—rather good experience. Real life has to do with this: Only moments when you are experiencing joy and freedom. Think about that for a few moments. Only that is real life!

Reminds me of a young lady who made this toast at a dinner. I have never forgotten it. It was not humorous—but it left a vivid impression on me. In a quiet voice she said, "May you live every day that you live." Even with the most fortunate of people, if they had a clock that could list such moments of real life, I doubt that such moments would add up to very many.

So the Hidden Bible promises "long life" here. In other words, long or many such moments.

And those moments will begin to come into your life, moments of joy and freedom. First they will be just moments—if you take this particular statement of Higher Law, claim it and really open yourself to it. Yes, first they will be just moments, then lengthening moments. The intervals in between will grow shorter, and finally such good moments will stay with you permanently. And so the Hidden Bible here promises that kind of "long life." It is worth investigating.

You will still do outer things in this new life— but without effort, rather with joy. The things you do, you will do with joy—against the things you do now, with dullness. They will change as time goes on; and more important, new things also will come your way to do. Just living off the calendar is not "long life." Just being an octogenarian for an octogenarian's sake is not joyous —if you are bedridden or lonely.

Should you "milk" this one promise for all that it is worth, your health would improve tremendously—over and above all the vitamins you are now taking for that purpose. Your job would become thrilling, where it has been routine. Relations with others would become

334 THE BIBLE AS THE STORY OF YOU

happy, truly happy. That is "long life." "With long life will I satisfy him. . . ." who calls on God for this. This is what the statement is saying. Yes, in those ways in which your present life leaves you unsatisfied.

Now for one more, Psalms again, the 25th Psalm: 9th verse, "The meek will He guide in judgment: and the meek will He teach His way." "Meek" is your polar word. To be meek means to give all power unto God. It does not mean being a doormat. You know, "Too late now, but if you could possibly see your way clear God—help me." Or, "God can, but I am a miserable sinner, a worm of the dust and a child of iniquity." Is that not ridiculous? Some well-meaning theologian thought that up centuries after Jesus Christ. It is not in the Bible. The only description Jesus ever gave of you and me was, "Children of The Highest." And that is the greatest thing possible to be said about us.

Another way of not being meek is to go to God—all right enough. Never saying it is too late or describing yourself in any negative fashion. But still, not being meek, because when you go to God—you tell Him how to do it. That is your mistake. So you never get through or pass the required condition—meekness. "The meek will He guide in judgment. . . ." Therefore, when you want to make that right decision, make that right choice—remember, "The meek will He guide in judgment. . . ." He does not get through to those people, you know, who buy a ticket first, and then ask God if they should go. Notice how seemingly He always says, "Yes," for such people. But you may question whether the "yes" was from God!

". . . And the meek will He teach his way," the Bible promise goes on to say. What we all want in our hearts is God's way, because we know it leads to the "life more abundant" right now. Sometimes we fool ourselves. We think we will be satisfied with certain material things. But in our heart we are really after MORE OF GOD. For having more of Him, the outer things are added.

Now where does meekness come in here? You surely do not have it when you say, "I won't get it because I am not good enough yet." Why? You are still standing on the outside of this promise—you are not meek. You should be saying, "Yes, God can and will do it, because He cares about me always." Then you are meek.

If you have found this subject interesting, you still will not get anything from it until you try out these promises. Not just these given in this segment. You have considered them somewhat with me already. Look for new promises. And with them—new and thrilling interest Godward. They will help you respond as never before, by allowing you to give all power unto God to bring another miracle into your life!

Spiritual Meditation

Many people would be quite surprised to hear that—as far as the Judaeo-Christian Bible is concerned—there are two Bibles. The ordinary one, whichever version, is one Bible. Then there is another, the Hidden Bible, which lies between the lines, so to speak.

The Hidden Bible is discovered only through understanding the key or polar words and phrases; which are found—not only in the parables, allegories, historical sections and prophecies—but also in the individual promises. These promises are actually statements of Divine Law or Higher Law.

It is this Hidden Bible that heals the body, melts away our difficulties and teaches us the things that matter. It gives us real knowledge—not just intellectual doctrine, dogma and creed. Yes, definite knowledge, which we can realize, and when we do—our lives are changed to that degree from that moment henceforth.

Just as it is the negative suggestion we accept, which brings harm into our lives; even so, it is the instruction from the Hidden Bible, which we accept through realization, that changes our lives for the better. The Hidden Bible does just that. It puts the new thing into our subconscious, and it goes right to work.

The outer history of the Bible, when read only as history—the sacking of Jerusalem three times, for example—does not do anything for you. But the Hidden Bible does. It keeps you from mistakes, heals you and dissolves your fears.

"The meek will He guide in judgment: and the meek will He teach His way."

Psalm 25:9